Math Competition Books Serie

The Mass Points Method

Yongcheng Chen, Ph.D.

http://www.mymathcounts.com/index.php

This book introduces a powerful problem solving technique – the mass points method. The book can be used by students preparing for math competitions such as Mathcounts, AMC 10/12/AIME.

Copyright © 2016, 2017, 2020, 2021 by mymathcounts.com
All rights reserved. Printed in the United States of America

Reproduction of any portion of this book without the written permission of the authors is strictly prohibited, except as may be expressly permitted by the U.S. Copyright Act.

ISBN-13: 978-1542458702
ISBN-10: 1542458706

Please contact mymathcounts@gmail.com for suggestions, corrections, or clarifications.

To My Wife, GUILING,
Whose Assistance and Encouragement
Make this Book Possible

ACKNOWLEDGEMENTS

We would like to thank Mr. Thomas Rike, the author of "A Decade of the Berkeley Math Circle – the American Experience". This book was inspired by his article: "Mass Point Geometry".

Table of Contents

1. Terms and Properties — 1

2. Direct Application of Mass Points — 20

3. Removing Line Segments — 47

4. Splitting Mass Points — 62

5. Length and Area Problems — 77

6. Quadrilaterals and Space Problems — 122

Index — 147

This page is intentionally left blank.

The Mass Points Method — Chapter 1. Terms and Properties

Chapter 1. Terms and Properties

1. Terms

The Mass Points Method

The mass points method is a technique that simplifies solving problems involving ratios of line segments in a geometric figure. When this method is used to solve the problem, it is much faster and easier than other methods such as proportion relationship, auxiliary line drawing, or area addition. In many cases when you use this method, you can explain your solution verbally without pen and paper.

Mass point

A mass point is a point (vertex or a point of intersection) without volume but with mass.

In this book, the masses of points *A, B,* and *C* are written as m_A, m_B, and m_C, respectively, in any equation. ⓝ will be used to denote the mass at a certain point in a figure. For example, ① indicates that the mass of the point is 1 unit.

Center of Mass

The center of mass is a point in an object where its mass is concentrated. When an object is supported at its center of mass, the object is balanced.

If two points each with mass are connected by a massless rod, the rod will balance at the center of mass. The center of mass will lie along the rod connecting the two masses and sit closer to the heavier point. If the masses of the two points are equal, then the center of mass will be exactly halfway between them. In general, the center of mass is the weighted average of the positions of each object, weighted by the mass of that object.

The Mass Points Method **Chapter 1. Terms and Properties**

2. Properties

Property 1 (Seesaw Relationship)

We have two **mass points** A and B. Let AC denote the length between points A and C and BC denote the length between points B and C. AB is called the **lever**. Point C, where the lever balances on, is called the **fulcrum**, and also the **center of mass**. It follows that:

$$m_A \times AC = m_B \times BC \qquad (1)$$

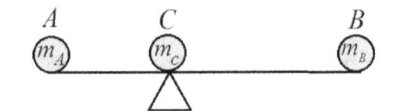

and $m_A + m_B = m_C \qquad (2)$

The lengths are inversely proportional to their masses.

Given the two masses m_A and m_B, we can compute $\dfrac{AC}{BC}$, the ratio of the lengths.

$$\frac{AC}{BC} = \frac{m_B}{m_A} \qquad (3)$$

$$\frac{AC}{AB} = \frac{m_B}{m_A + m_B} = \frac{m_B}{m_C} \qquad (4)$$

$$\frac{BC}{AB} = \frac{m_A}{m_A + m_B} = \frac{m_A}{m_C} \qquad (5)$$

If we are able to find the value of the two masses m_A and m_B, then we can find the ratio of certain line segments. This is the key point of the mass points method.

Property 2. Let the center of mass of m_A and m_B be located at P, with the mass m_P. The center of mass of m_P and m_D, ie. point C, with the mass m_C, located on the line PD, is also the center of mass of m_A, m_B, and m_D.

The Mass Points Method   Chapter 1. Terms and Properties

Property 3. If the center of mass of m_A, m_B, and m_D is located at C (with mass m_C), then P (with the mass m_p), the point of intersection between lines AC and BD is the center of mass of m_B and m_D.

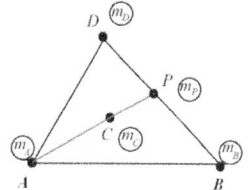

Property 4. Line segments AC and BD meet at point E. Given m_A, m_B, m_C, m_D, the masses of points A, B, C, and D, we have the following relationship: $m_A + m_C = m_B + m_D$.

Proof:
E is the center of mass for line segment AC. So we have
$m_E = m_A + m_C$

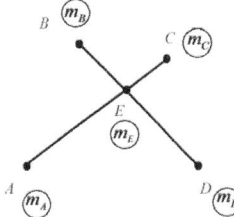

E is also the center of mass for line segment BD. So we have
$m_E = m_B + m_D$.

Thus we have $m_A + m_C = m_B + m_D$

Property 5. $ABCD$ is a parallelogram. Given m_A, m_B, m_C, m_D, the masses of four vertices A, B, C, and D, we have the following relationship:
$m_A + m_C = m_B + m_D$.

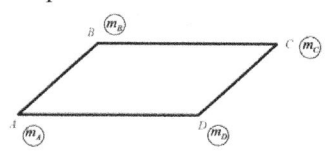

Proof:
We draw AC and BD, the diagonals of $ABCD$. AC and BD meet at point E.

Now we look at the line segment AC. Since E is the midpoint of AC, we have
$m_E = m_A + m_C$

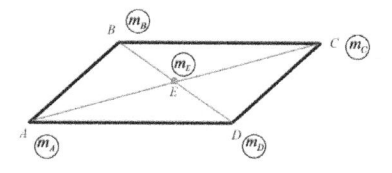

Now we look at the line segment BD. Since E is the midpoint of BD, we have

$m_E = m_B + m_D$.

Thus we have $m_A + m_C = m_B + m_D$

3. Cevian lines in a triangle

A **Cevian line** in a triangle is a line segment drawn from any vertex to the opposite side.

For example, *AX, BY, CZ* are Cevian lines.

Three distinct lines on a plane are said to be concurrent if they all go through the same point.

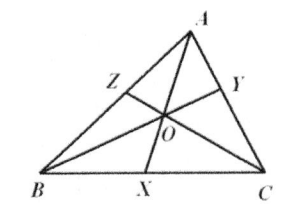

Ceva's Theorem If the cevians *AX, BY* and *CZ* of $\triangle ABC$ are concurrent, then
$$\frac{AZ}{ZB} \cdot \frac{BX}{XC} \cdot \frac{CY}{YA} = 1.$$

Proof:
Method 1:
Draw *GH//BC* through A to meet the extensions of *CZ* and *BY* at *G* and *H*, respectively.

By similar triangles, we have
$\dfrac{CY}{AY} = \dfrac{BC}{AH}$; $\dfrac{AZ}{BZ} = \dfrac{GA}{BC}$;

$\dfrac{BX}{AH} = \dfrac{OX}{AO}$; and $\dfrac{CX}{AG} = \dfrac{OX}{AO}$

$\therefore \quad \dfrac{BX}{CX} = \dfrac{AH}{GA}$.

$\therefore \quad \dfrac{CY}{AY} \cdot \dfrac{AZ}{BZ} \cdot \dfrac{BX}{CX} = \dfrac{BC}{AH} \cdot \dfrac{GA}{BC} \cdot \dfrac{AH}{GA} = 1$

Method 2:
Let $S_{\triangle AOB}=S_1$, $S_{\triangle BOC}=S_2$, $S_{\triangle COA}=S_3$.
Then

$$\frac{AZ}{ZB}=\frac{S_3}{S_2} \quad (1)$$

$$\frac{BX}{XC}=\frac{S_1}{S_3} \quad (2)$$

$$\frac{CY}{YA}=\frac{S_2}{S_1} \quad (3)$$

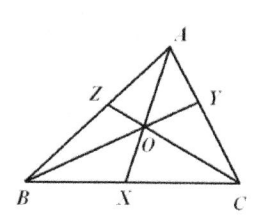

$(1) \times (2) \times (3)$: $\dfrac{AZ}{ZB} \cdot \dfrac{BX}{XC} \cdot \dfrac{CY}{YA}=1$.

Converse of Ceva' Theorem

If $\dfrac{AZ}{ZB} \cdot \dfrac{BX}{XC} \cdot \dfrac{CY}{YA}=1$, then X, Y and Z are concurrent.

Ceva's theorem and its converse provide us with a criterion to determine whether three given cevians are concurrent.

4. Typical Problems that can be solved using the mass points method:

(1) In the figures below, *AE* and *BD* are Cevian lines of the triangle *ABC*. There are also four pairs of line segments: *AM* and *ME*; *BM* and *MD*; *AD* and *DC*; *BE* and *EC*. If we know the ratios of any **two** pairs, we can use the mass points method to determine the other two ratios.

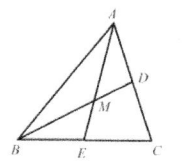

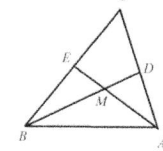

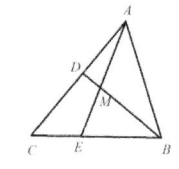

The Mass Points Method   Chapter 1. Terms and Properties

(2) In the figures below, we can draw an auxiliary line and then apply the mass points method.

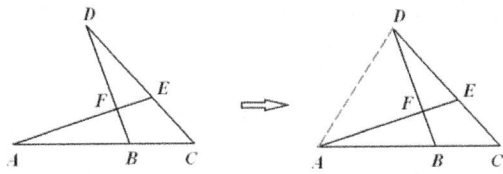

(3) If we have two cevian lines coming from one vertex, we can remove one cevian line at a time and then apply the mass points method.

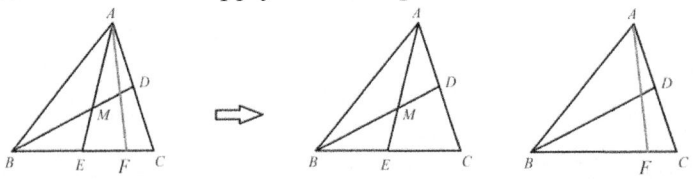

(4) For problems that involve *EF*, the transversal in the figure below, we can split the mass at vertex A as follows:

Mass at the vertex (A) can be split as $m_A = m_{A_{AB}} + m_{A_{AC}}$.

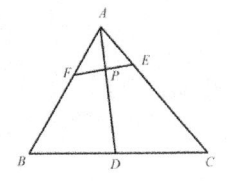

When we apply the mass points method to line *AB*, we use $m_{A_{AB}}$ and m_B.

When we apply the mass points method to line *AC*, we use $m_{A_{AC}}$ and m_C.

When we apply the mass points method to line *AD*, we use m_A and m_D.

5. Ways to label line segment lengths in the mass points method

To use the mass points method, we need to know at least two ratios of line segment lengths. The following show 4 general ways on how to find and label the lengths of line segments.

The Mass Points Method   **Chapter 1. Terms and Properties**

Case 1: In △ABC, AD is the median on BC. Point F lies on BC and AC, respectively. $\frac{AE}{ED} = \frac{1}{3}$.

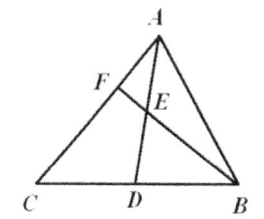

Since AD is the median on BC, we know that CD = DB. Since their ratio is 1 : 1, we can label CD as 1 and DB as 1.

Since $\frac{AE}{ED} = \frac{1}{3}$, we can label AE as 1 and ED as 3.

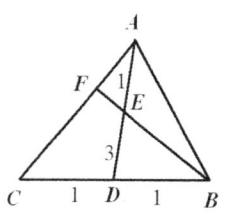

Case 2: In △ABC, AD is the angle bisector of ∠A. AC = 3, AB = 6.

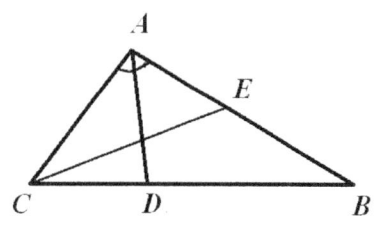

Since AD is the angle bisector, we know that $\frac{AC}{AB} = \frac{CD}{BD} = \frac{3}{6} = \frac{1}{2}$. So we can label CD as 1 and BD as 2.

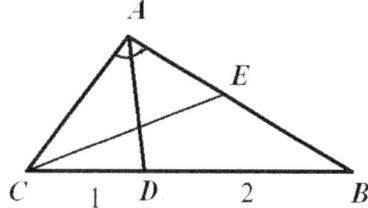

7

The Mass Points Method   **Chapter 1. Terms and Properties**

Case 3: AD divides $\triangle ABC$ into two triangles with the areas of $S_{\triangle ACD} = 6$, and $S_{\triangle ABD} = 15$.

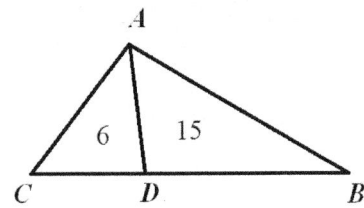

Since $\dfrac{S_{\triangle ACD}}{S_{\triangle ABD}} = \dfrac{6}{15} = \dfrac{2}{5} = \dfrac{\frac{1}{2} CD \times h}{\frac{1}{2} AD \times h} = \dfrac{CD}{BD}$, we know that $\dfrac{CD}{BD} = \dfrac{2}{5}$. So we can label CD as 2 and DB as 5.

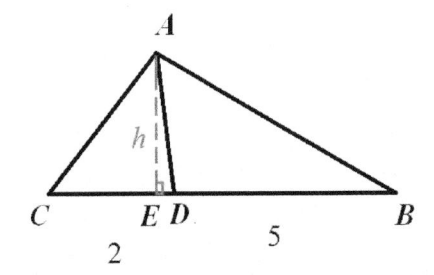

Case 4: In $\triangle ABC$, E and F are points on BC and AC, respectively, such that $AB \,/\!/\, EF$ with $\dfrac{AF}{FC} = \dfrac{3}{2}$

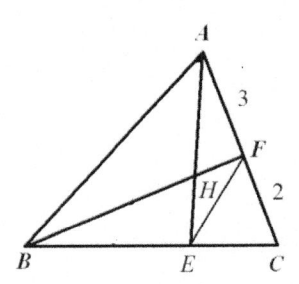

Since $AB \,/\!/\, EF$, we know that $\dfrac{AF}{FC} = \dfrac{BE}{EC} = \dfrac{3}{2}$. The ratio $\dfrac{BE}{EC} = \dfrac{3}{2}$. So we can label BE as 3 and EC as 2.

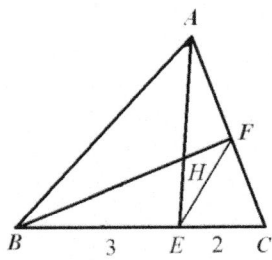

The Mass Points Method   Chapter 1. Terms and Properties

Example 1. Find m_E.

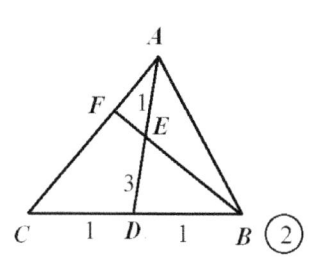

Solution: 16.

Taking a look at the segment BC, we have
$$m_C \times CD = m_B \times DB \implies m_C \times 1 = 2 \times 1 \implies m_C = 2$$

We know that D is the center of mass of B and C.
Therefore, $m_D = m_B + m_C = 2 + 2 = 4$.

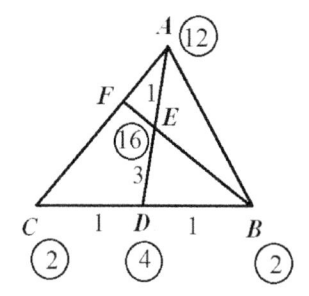

Now, we take a look at the segment AD.
$$m_D \times ED = m_A \times AE \implies 4 \times 3 = m_A \times 1 \implies m_A = 12$$
$$m_E = m_A + m_D = 12 + 4 = 16.$$

Example 2. Find $\dfrac{FE}{EB}$.

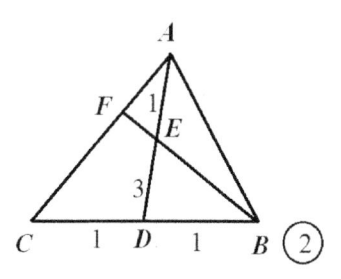

Solution: $\dfrac{1}{7}$.

$$\dfrac{FE}{EB} = \dfrac{m_B}{m_F} \qquad (1)$$

Taking look at the segment AD, we have
$$m_D \times ED = m_A \times AE \implies 4 \times 3 = m_A \times 1 \implies m_A = 12$$
$$m_F = m_A + m_C = 12 + 2 = 14.$$

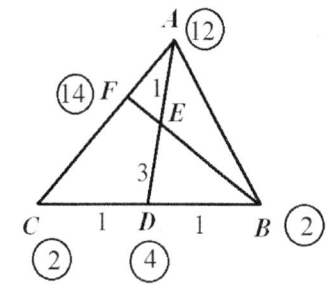

Since $m_F = m_A + m_C = 12 + 2 = 14$.
Plugging the values of m_F and m_B in (1) gives us
$$\dfrac{FE}{EB} = \dfrac{m_B}{m_F} = \dfrac{2}{14} = \dfrac{1}{7}.$$

The Mass Points Method　　　　　　　　**Chapter 1. Terms and Properties**

Example 3. Find $\dfrac{AD}{AC}$.

Solution: $\dfrac{5}{8}$.

$\dfrac{AD}{AC} = \dfrac{m_C}{m_D}$.

Taking a look at the segment AB, we have
$m_A \times AE = m_B \times BE \quad \Rightarrow \quad m_A \times 2 = 2 \times 3 \quad \Rightarrow \quad m_A = 3$

We know that D is the center of mass of A and C, so $m_D = m_A + m_C = 3 + 5 = 8$.

$\dfrac{AD}{AC} = \dfrac{m_C}{m_D} = \dfrac{5}{8}$.

Example 4. As shown in the figure, D and E are points on BC of triangle ABC such that $BD : DE : EC = 1 : 1 : 1$. The median BF meets AD and AE at G and H respectively and is divided into the lengths of BG, GH, HF. Find $\dfrac{AG}{GD}$.

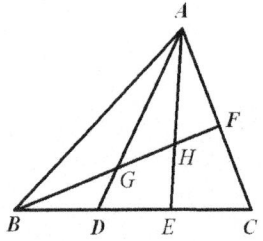

Solution: 3.

$\dfrac{AG}{GD} = \dfrac{m_D}{m_A}$

We remove the segment AE and label each line segment as shown in the figure to the right.

We assign a mass of 1 to point C.

$m_B \times 1 = m_C \times 2 \quad \Rightarrow \quad m_B = 2$.

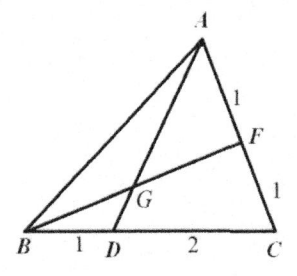

The Mass Points Method   **Chapter 1. Terms and Properties**

$m_D = m_B + m_C = 2 + 1 = 3$.

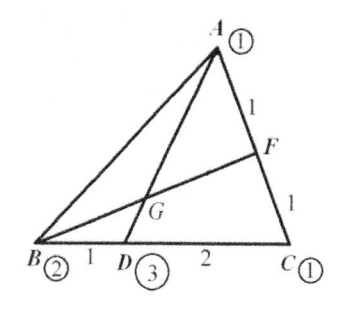

Now we take a look at line AC:

$m_A \times 1 = m_C \times 1 \Rightarrow \quad m_A = 1$.

$m_G = m_A + m_D = 1 + 3 = 4$

$\dfrac{AG}{GD} = \dfrac{m_D}{m_A} = \dfrac{3}{1} = 3$.

Example 5. Find m_A if $m_B = 2$, $m_F = 7$, $m_C = 3$, and $m_E = 5$.

Solution: 7.

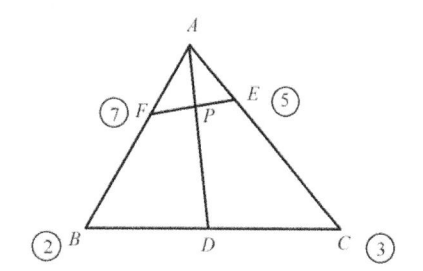

$m_{A_{AB}} = m_F - m_B = 7 - 2 = 5$.

$m_{A_{AC}} = m_E - m_C = 5 - 3 = 2$

$m_A = m_{A_{AB}} + m_{A_{AC}} = 5 + 2 = 7$

Example 6. Find $\dfrac{AP}{PD}$ if $m_B = 2$, $m_F = 7$, $m_C = 3$, and $m_E = 5$.

Solution: $\dfrac{5}{7}$.

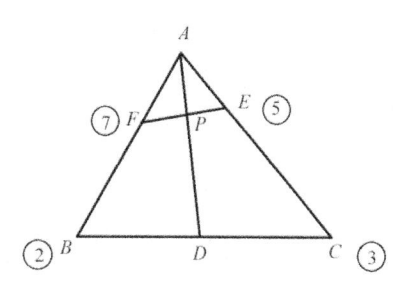

$\dfrac{AP}{PD} = \dfrac{m_D}{m_A}$

$m_{A_{AB}} = m_F - m_B = 7 - 2 = 5$.

$m_{A_{AC}} = m_E - m_C = 5 - 3 = 2$

$m_A = m_{A_{AB}} + m_{A_{AC}} = 5 + 2 = 7$.

$m_D = m_B + m_C = 2 + 3 = 5$

$\dfrac{AP}{PD} = \dfrac{m_D}{m_A} = \dfrac{5}{7}$.

Example 7. (Menelaus' Theorem) A line intersects the sides or extension of the sides *AB, BC* and *CA* of $\triangle ABC$ at *X, Y* and *Z*, respectively. The following holds $\dfrac{AX}{BX} \cdot \dfrac{BY}{CY} \cdot \dfrac{CZ}{AZ} = 1$.

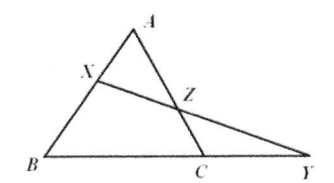

Proof:
Method 1:

$$\dfrac{AX}{BX} = \dfrac{m_B}{m_A} \quad (1)$$

$$\dfrac{BY}{CY} = \dfrac{m_C}{m_B} \quad (2)$$

$$\dfrac{CZ}{AZ} = \dfrac{m_A}{m_C} \quad (3)$$

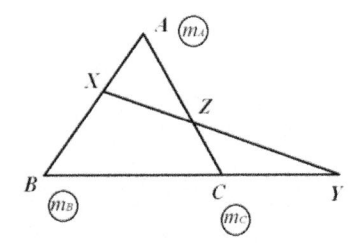

(1) × (2) × (3):

$$\dfrac{AX}{BX} \cdot \dfrac{BY}{CY} \cdot \dfrac{CZ}{AZ} = \dfrac{m_B}{m_A} \cdot \dfrac{m_C}{m_B} \cdot \dfrac{m_A}{m_C} = 1.$$

Method 2:
Draw *CG*//*XY* to meet *AB* at *G*.

Since $\triangle BYX \sim \triangle BCG$, we have $\dfrac{BY}{CY} = \dfrac{BX}{GX}$ (1)

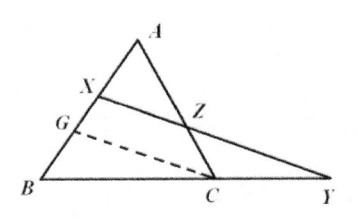

Since $\triangle AGC \sim \triangle AXZ$, we have $\dfrac{CZ}{AZ} = \dfrac{GX}{AX}$ (2)

(1) × (2): $\dfrac{BY}{CY} \times \dfrac{CZ}{AZ} = \dfrac{BX}{GX} \times \dfrac{GX}{AX} = \dfrac{BX}{AX}$, or $\dfrac{AX}{BX} \cdot \dfrac{BY}{CY} \cdot \dfrac{CZ}{AZ} = 1$.

The Mass Points Method — Chapter 1. Terms and Properties

Example 8. (Ceva's Theorem) If the cevians AX, BY and CZ of $\triangle ABC$ are concurrent, then $\dfrac{AZ}{ZB} \cdot \dfrac{BX}{XC} \cdot \dfrac{CY}{YA} = 1$.

Proof:

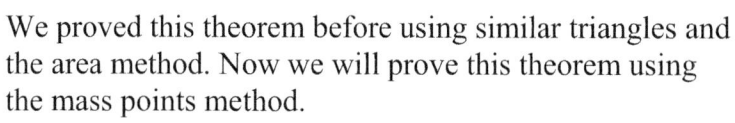

We proved this theorem before using similar triangles and the area method. Now we will prove this theorem using the mass points method.

$$\frac{AZ}{ZB} = \frac{m_B}{m_A} \qquad (1)$$

$$\frac{BX}{XC} = \frac{m_C}{m_B} \qquad (2)$$

$$\frac{CY}{YA} = \frac{m_A}{m_C} \qquad (3)$$

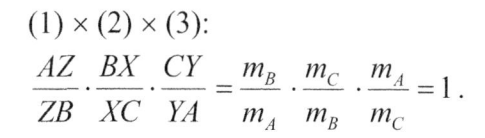

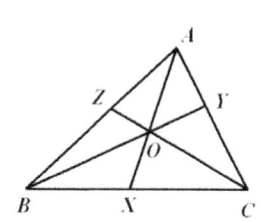

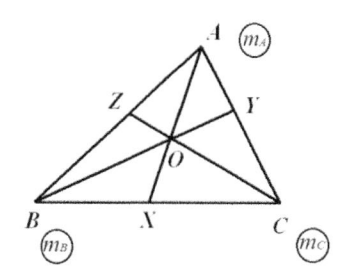

(1) × (2) × (3):

$$\frac{AZ}{ZB} \cdot \frac{BX}{XC} \cdot \frac{CY}{YA} = \frac{m_B}{m_A} \cdot \frac{m_C}{m_B} \cdot \frac{m_A}{m_C} = 1.$$

The Mass Points Method — Chapter 1. Terms and Properties

Chapter 1. Problems

Problem 1. Find m_F.

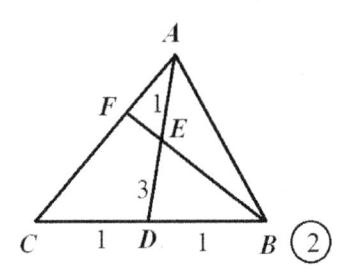

Problem 2. Find $\dfrac{AE}{AD}$.

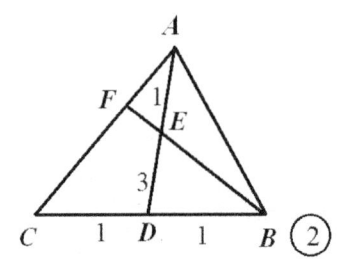

Problem 3. Find $\dfrac{BF}{BD}$.

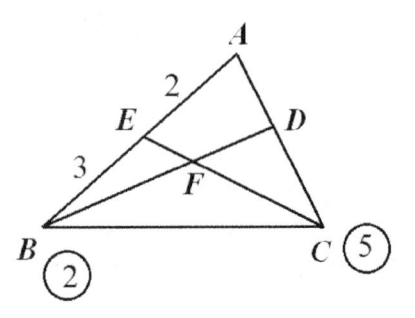

Problem 4. As shown in the figure, D and E are points on BC of triangle ABC such that $BD : DE : EC = 1 : 1 : 1$. The median BF meets AD and AE at G and H respectively and is divided into the lengths of BG, GH, HF. Find $\dfrac{FH}{FB}$.

Problem 5. Find m_A if $m_B = 5$, $m_F = 7$, $m_C = 3$, and $m_E = 8$.

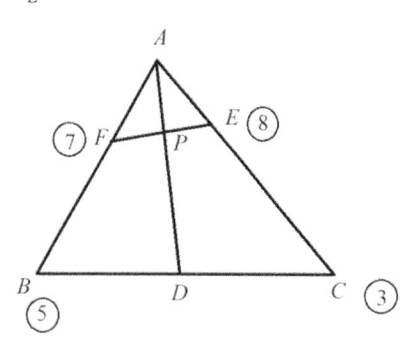

Problem 6. Find $\dfrac{AP}{AD}$ if $m_B = 5$, $m_F = 7$, $m_C = 3$, and $m_E = 8$.

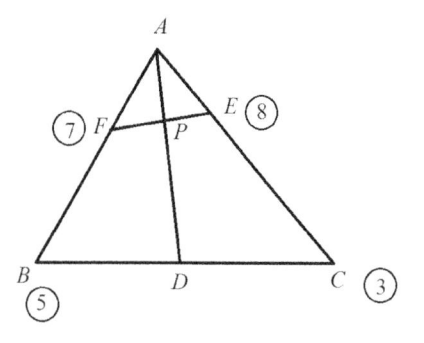

Problem 7. As shown in the figure, AM is the median of $\triangle ABC$. Line segment PQ meets AB at P, AC at Q, and AM at N such that $PN = NQ$. Show $PQ // BC$.

The Mass Points Method   Chapter 1. Terms and Properties

Chapter 1. Solutions

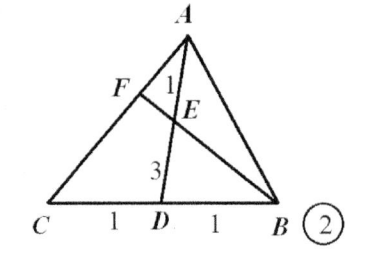

Problem 1. Solution: 14.

Taking a look at the segment BC, we have
$$m_C \times CD = m_B \times DB \implies m_C \times 1 = 2 \times 1 \implies$$
$$m_C = 2$$

We know that D is the center of mass of B and C, so $m_D = m_B + m_C = 2 + 2 = 4$.

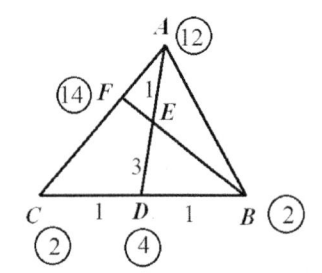

Now taking a look at the segment AD, we have
$$m_D \times ED = m_A \times AE \implies 4 \times 3 = m_A \times 1 \implies m_A = 12$$
$$m_F = m_A + m_C = 12 + 2 = 14.$$

Problem 2. Solution: 16. 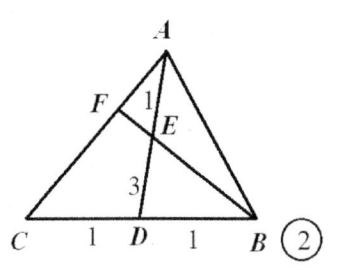
$$\frac{AE}{AD} = \frac{m_D}{m_E} \quad (1)$$

Taking a look at the segment BC, we have
$$m_C \times CD = m_B \times DB \implies m_C \times 1 = 2 \times 1 \implies m_C = 2$$

We know that D is the center of mass of B and C, so $m_D = m_B + m_C = 2 + 2 = 4$.

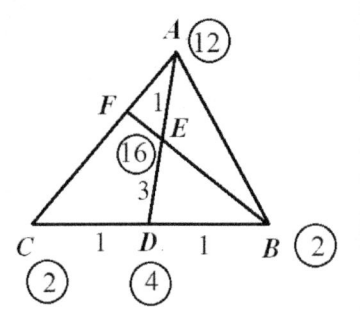

Now taking a look at the segment AD, we have
$$m_D \times ED = m_A \times AE \implies 4 \times 3 = m_A \times 1 \implies$$
$$m_A = 12$$
$$m_E = m_A + m_D = 12 + 4 = 16.$$

Plugging the values of m_E and m_D in (1) gives us
$$\frac{AE}{AD} = \frac{m_D}{m_E} = \frac{4}{16} = \frac{1}{4}.$$

Problem 3. Solution: $\dfrac{4}{5}$.

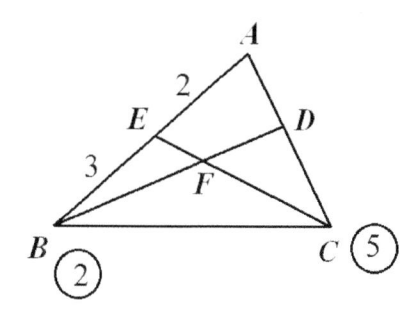

$$\dfrac{BF}{BD} = \dfrac{m_D}{m_F} \quad (1)$$

Taking a look at segment AB, we have

$$m_A \times AE = m_B \times BE \quad \Rightarrow \quad m_A \times 2 = 2 \times 3 \quad \Rightarrow$$

$$m_A = 3$$

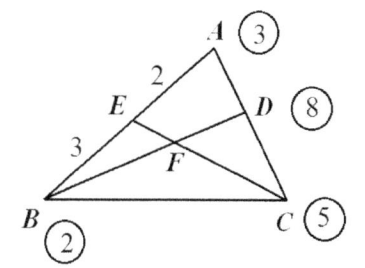

We know that D is the center of mass of B and C, so $m_D = m_A + m_C = 3 + 5 = 8$.

$$\dfrac{BF}{BD} = \dfrac{m_D}{m_F} = \dfrac{8}{10} = \dfrac{4}{5}.$$

Problem 4. Solution: $\dfrac{1}{5}$.

$$\dfrac{FH}{FB} = \dfrac{m_B}{m_H}$$

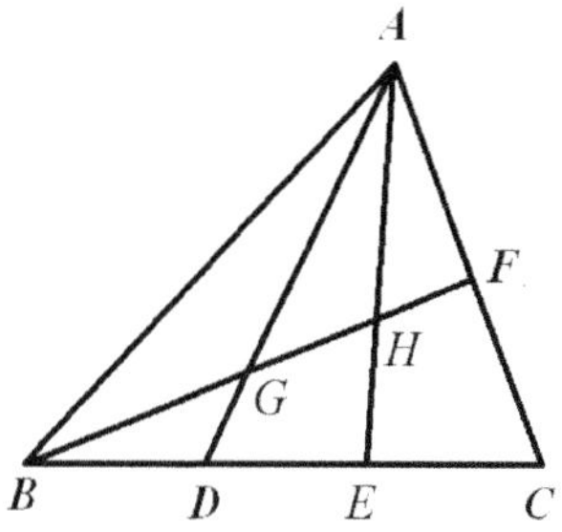

Remove the segment AD and label each line segment as shown.

Now, assign a mass of 2 to point C.

$$m_B \times BE = m_C \times EC \quad \Rightarrow$$

$$m_B \times 2 = 2 \times 1 \quad \Rightarrow \quad m_B = 1.$$

$$m_D = m_B + m_C = 2 + 1 = 3.$$

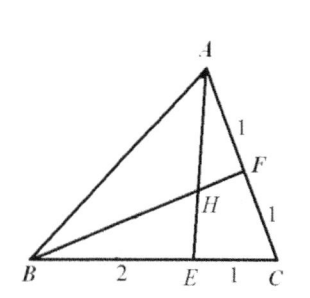

Taking a look at line AC, we have

$$m_A \times AF = m_C \times FC \Rightarrow \quad m_A \times 1 = 2 \times 1 \quad \Rightarrow \quad m_A = 2.$$

$$m_F = m_A + m_C = 2 + 2 = 4.$$

$$m_H = m_B + m_F = 1 + 4 = 5$$

The Mass Points Method **Chapter 1. Terms and Properties**

$$\frac{FH}{FB} = \frac{m_B}{m_H} = \frac{1}{5}.$$

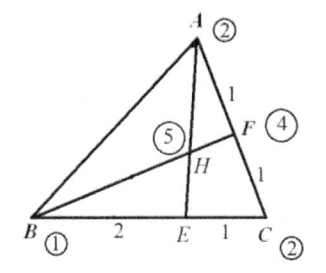

Problem 5. Solution: 7.
$$m_{A_{AB}} = m_F - m_B = 7 - 5 = 2.$$
$$m_{A_{AC}} = m_E - m_C = 8 - 3 = 5$$
$$m_A = m_{A_{AB}} + m_{A_{AC}} = 2 + 5 = 7$$

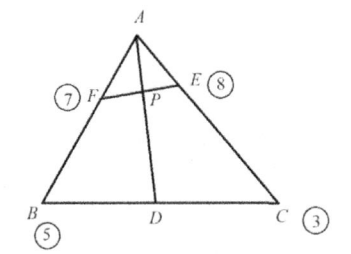

Problem 6. Solution: $\frac{8}{15}$.

$$\frac{AP}{AD} = \frac{m_D}{m_P}$$
$$m_{A_{AB}} = m_F - m_B = 7 - 5 = 2.$$
$$m_{A_{AC}} = m_E - m_C = 8 - 3 = 5$$
$$m_A = m_{A_{AB}} + m_{A_{AC}} = 2 + 5 = 7$$
$$m_D = m_B + m_C = 5 + 3 = 8$$
$$m_P = m_F + m_E = 7 + 8 = 15$$

$$\frac{AP}{AD} = \frac{m_D}{m_P} = \frac{8}{15}.$$

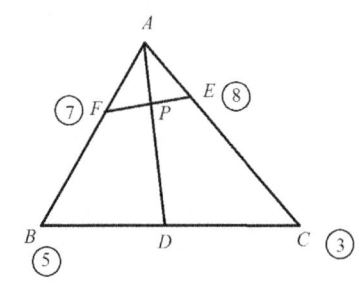

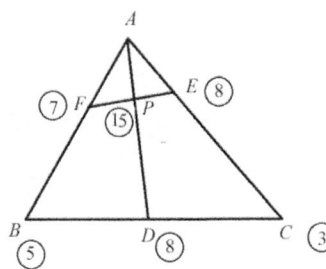

Problem 7. Proof:
Method 1:

We know that $PQ // BC$ if $\frac{AP}{AB} = \frac{AQ}{AC}$.

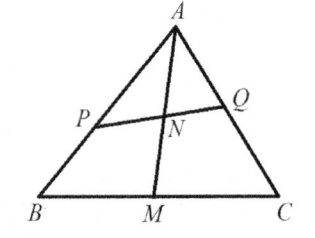

We assign $m_B = 1$ and get $m_C = 1$ and $m_M = 2$.

18

$$\frac{AP}{AB} = \frac{m_B}{m_P} = \frac{1}{m_P} \quad (1)$$

$$\frac{AQ}{AC} = \frac{m_C}{m_Q} = \frac{1}{m_Q} \quad (2)$$

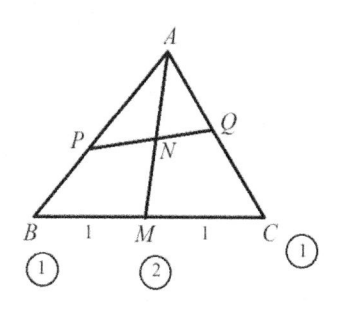

Since $PN = NQ$, $m_P = m_Q$

Thus $\dfrac{AP}{AB} = \dfrac{AQ}{AC}$ and $PQ // BC$.

Method 2:

We are given that $PN = NQ$. Since $BM = CM$, $S_{\triangle ABM} = S_{\triangle ACM}$.

Applying (9.1) to $\triangle APN$ and $\triangle ABM$, we have

$$\frac{S_{\triangle APN}}{S_{\triangle AQN}} = \frac{S_{\triangle ABM}}{S_{\triangle ACM}} = 1 \quad \Rightarrow \quad \frac{S_{\triangle APN}}{S_{\triangle ABM}} = \frac{S_{\triangle AQN}}{S_{\triangle ACM}} \quad \Rightarrow \quad \frac{AP \times AN}{AB \times AM} = \frac{AN \times AQ}{AM \times AC}$$

$$\Rightarrow \quad \frac{AP}{AB} = \frac{AQ}{AC}.$$

Thus $PQ // BC$.

The Mass Points Method   Chapter 2. Direct Application of Mass Points

Chapter 2. Direct Application of Mass Points

Example 1. In $\triangle ABC$, AD is the median on BC. Point F lies on BF and AC. If AD and BF intersect at E so that $\dfrac{AE}{ED} = \dfrac{1}{3}$, what is $\dfrac{AF}{FC}$? Express your answer as a common fraction.

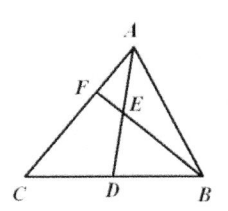

Solution: $\dfrac{1}{6}$.

$\dfrac{AF}{FC} = \dfrac{m_C}{m_A}$.

Step 1:
We label the length of each line segment as shown.

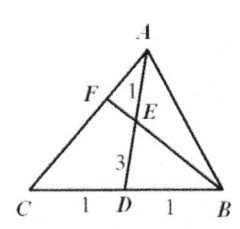

Since we are given that $\dfrac{AE}{ED} = \dfrac{1}{3}$ and we're only concerned about finding the ratio of $\dfrac{AF}{FC}$, we can label the length of AE as 1 and ED as 3.

Since AD is the median on BC, we know that $CD = DB$ or $\dfrac{CD}{DB} = \dfrac{1}{1}$ and we can then both CD and DB as 1.

Step 2:
Let the masses in each point be m_A, m_B, m_C, and m_D, respectively.

We can get $\dfrac{AF}{FC}$ from m_A and m_C.

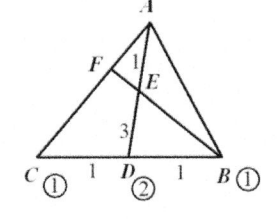

Let's assign a mass of 1 to point C.

Note:

(1) This number can be randomly assigned. But it is better you choose the number such that (a) it is easy to compute

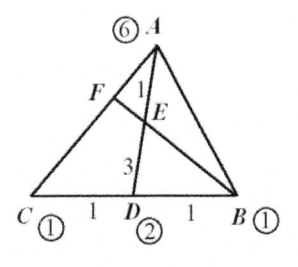

20

The Mass Points Method   Chapter 2. Direct Application of Mass Points

other masses and (b) you will avoid a fraction in your calculation.

(2) You can only assign one mass point a value. All others will be calculated based on that value using the seesaw formulas.

We take a look at the segment BC. We know that D is the center of mass of B and C, so

$m_C \times CD = m_B \times DB \Rightarrow 1 \times 1 = m_B \times 1$

$\Rightarrow m_B = 1$ and $m_D = m_B + m_C = 1 + 1 = 2$.

Now, we take a look at the segment AD.

We know that E is the center of mass of A and D, so $m_A \times AE = m_D \times DE$

$\Rightarrow m_A \times 1 = 2 \times 3 \Rightarrow m_A = 6$.

$$\frac{AF}{FC} = \frac{m_C}{m_A} = \frac{1}{6}.$$

Example 2. As shown in the figure, find $\dfrac{DE}{EC}$ if $\dfrac{AB}{BC} = \dfrac{DF}{FB} = 2$. Express your answer as a common fraction.

Solution: $\dfrac{4}{3}$.

$\dfrac{DE}{EC} = \dfrac{m_C}{m_D}$

We label the length of each line segment as shown.

Let's assign a mass of 1 to point A.

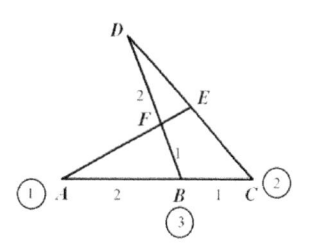

21

The Mass Points Method   Chapter 2. Direct Application of Mass Points

$m_A \times 2 = m_C \times 1$

$\Rightarrow \quad m_C = 2$ and $m_B = m_A + m_C = 1 + 2 = 3$.

Similarly, $m_D \times 2 = m_B \times 1 \Rightarrow m_D = \dfrac{3}{2}$.

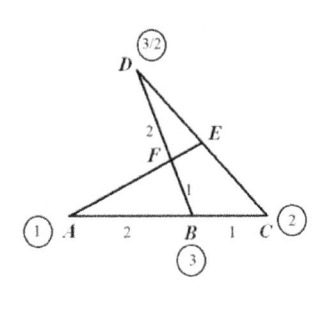

$\Rightarrow \quad \dfrac{DE}{EC} = \dfrac{m_C}{m_D} = \dfrac{2}{\dfrac{3}{2}} = \dfrac{4}{3}$.

Note: If we had assigned a mass of 2 to point A, we would not have gotten any fractional values for other masses.

Example 3. In $\triangle ABC$, side BC is divided by D in a ratio of 5 to 2 and BA is divided by E in a ratio of 3 to 4 as shown in Figure 1a. Find the ratios in which F divides the cevians AD and CE, i.e. find $EF : FC$ and $DF : FA$. Express your answer as a common fraction.

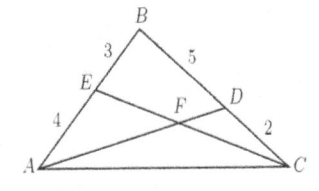

Solution: $\dfrac{10}{7}, \dfrac{3}{14}$.

(1) $\dfrac{EF}{FC} = \dfrac{m_C}{m_E}$.

Let's assign a mass of 4 to point B.

$m_B \times 3 = m_A \times 4 \quad \Rightarrow \quad m_A = 3$ and $m_E = m_A + m_B = 3 + 4 = 7$.

Similarly, $m_B \times 5 = m_C \times 2$

$\Rightarrow \quad m_C = 10$.

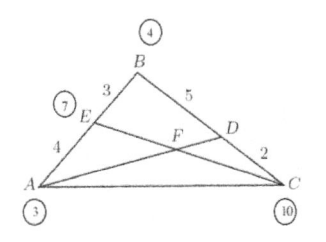

$\dfrac{EF}{FC} = \dfrac{m_C}{m_E} = \dfrac{10}{7}$.

(2) $\dfrac{DF}{FA} = \dfrac{m_A}{m_D}$.

22

The Mass Points Method   Chapter 2. Direct Application of Mass Points

$m_D = m_B + m_C = 4 + 10 = 14$.

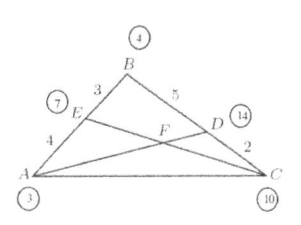

$\dfrac{DF}{FA} = \dfrac{m_A}{m_D} = \dfrac{3}{14}$.

Example 4. (Mathcounts) If $AB : BC = 1 : 4$ and $AF : DF = 5 : 4$, what is the ratio of DE to CD? Express your answer as a common fraction.

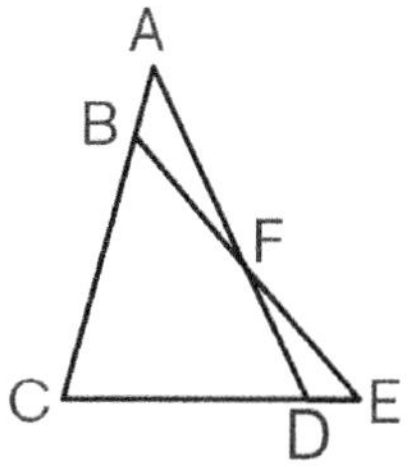

Solution: $\dfrac{1}{4}$.

$\dfrac{DE}{CD} = \dfrac{m_C}{m_E}$ (1)

We label the length of each line segment as shown.

Let the masses in each point be m_A, m_C, m_D, and m_E, respectively.

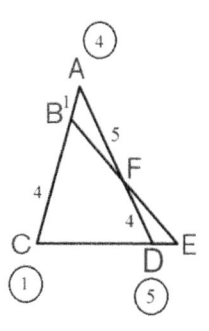

Let's assign a mass of 1 to point C.

$m_C \times 4 = m_A \times 1$

$\Rightarrow \quad m_A = 4$.

Taking a look at line segment AD, we have

$m_A \times 5 = m_D \times 4 \quad \Rightarrow \quad m_D = 5$.

Now taking a look at line segment CE, we have

$m_C \times CD = m_E \times DE$

$m_D = m_C + m_E \quad \Rightarrow \quad 5 = 1 + m_E \quad \Rightarrow \quad m_E = 4$.

Substituting m_C and m_E into (1):

$\dfrac{DE}{CD} = \dfrac{1}{4}$.

The Mass Points Method — Chapter 2. Direct Application of Mass Points

Example 5. (2004 AMC 10B Problem 20) In $\triangle ABC$, points D and E lie on BC and AC, respectively. If AD and BE intersect at T so that $\dfrac{AT}{DT} = 3$ and $\dfrac{BT}{ET} = 4$, what is $\dfrac{CD}{BD}$?

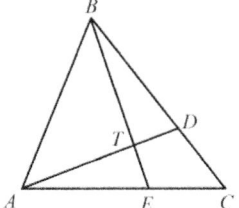

(A) $\dfrac{1}{8}$ (B) $\dfrac{2}{9}$ (C) $\dfrac{3}{10}$ (D) $\dfrac{4}{11}$ (E) $\dfrac{5}{12}$

Solution: $\dfrac{4}{11}$.

We will use a different method than the official solution to solve this problem.

$$\frac{CD}{BD} = \frac{m_B}{m_C} \qquad (1)$$

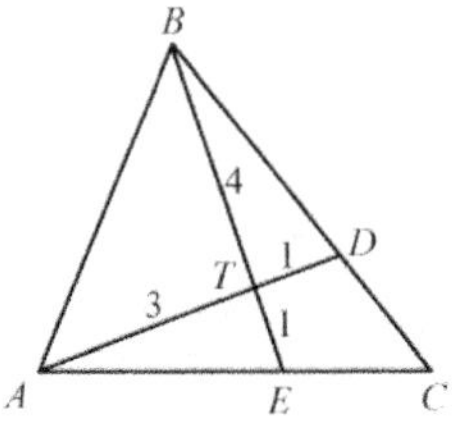

We label the length of each line segment as shown.

Let the masses in each point be m_A, m_B, m_C, m_D, m_E, and m_T, respectively.

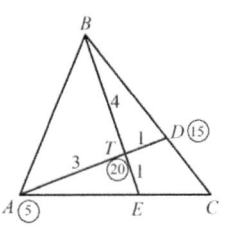

Let's assign a mass of 5 to point A.

$m_A \times 3 = m_D \times 1$

So $m_D = 15$ and $m_T = m_A + m_D = 5 + 15 = 20$.

Next, we determine m_B and m_E.

$m_B \times 4 = m_E \times 1$ \qquad (1)

$m_B + m_E = 20$ \qquad (2)

$m_B + 4m_B = 20 \Rightarrow \quad 5m_B = 20$

$\Rightarrow \quad m_B = 4$

and $m_E = 20 - 4 = 16$.

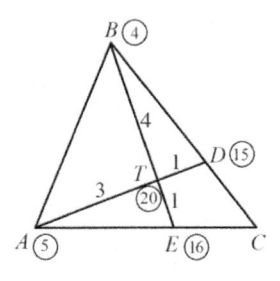

The Mass Points Method   **Chapter 2. Direct Application of Mass Points**

Next we determine m_C
$m_C + m_A = 16$
$\Rightarrow \quad m_C + 5 = 16$
$\Rightarrow \quad m_C = 11$.

The last step is to find the answer:
$$\frac{CD}{BD} = \frac{m_B}{m_C} = \frac{4}{11}.$$

Example 6. AD is the median of triangle ABC on BC. CF meets AD at E. Show that: $\dfrac{AE}{ED} = \dfrac{2AF}{FB}$.

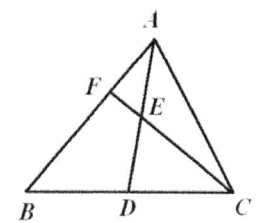

Solution:
$\dfrac{AF}{FB} = \dfrac{m_B}{m_A}$.

$\dfrac{AE}{ED} = \dfrac{m_D}{m_A}$.

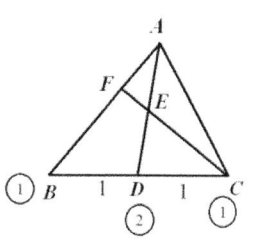

We label the length of each line segment as shown.

Let's assign a mass of 1 to point B.
$m_B \times 1 = m_C \times 1$
$\Rightarrow \quad m_C = 1$ and $m_D = m_B + m_C = 1 + 1 = 2$.

Next, we look at the line segment AB:
$m_A \times AF = m_B \times FB$
$\Rightarrow \dfrac{AF}{FB} = \dfrac{m_B}{m_A} = \dfrac{1}{m_A}$ (1)

25

Next, we look at the line segment AD:

$m_A \times AE = m_D \times ED \Rightarrow \dfrac{AE}{ED} = \dfrac{m_D}{m_A} = \dfrac{2}{m_A}$ (2)

$(1) \div (2)$: $\dfrac{AE}{ED} = \dfrac{2AF}{FB}$.

Example 7. (2011 National Team 9) In triangle ABC, point D is on segment AC with $AD : DC = 2 : 1$, and point E is on segment AB with $AE : EB = 2 : 3$. Segments EC and DB intersect at point K. What is $DK : KB$? Express your answer as a common fraction.

Solution: 2/9.

$\dfrac{DK}{KB} = \dfrac{m_B}{m_D}$.

We label the length of each line segment as shown.

Let the masses in each point be m_A, m_B, m_C, and m_D, respectively.

We assign a mass of 3 to point A.

$m_A \times 2 = m_C \times 1$

$\Rightarrow \quad m_C = 6$ and $m_D = m_A + m_C = 3 + 6 = 9$.

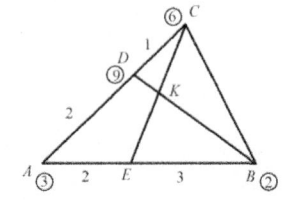

Next, we determine m_B.

$m_A \times 2 = m_B \times 3 \quad \Rightarrow \quad m_B = 2$.

Finally, we get $\dfrac{DK}{KB} = \dfrac{2}{9}$.

The Mass Points Method   **Chapter 2. Direct Application of Mass Points**

Example 8. As shown in the figure, G is the point where the three medians meet. Prove that $AG = \frac{2}{3} AD$.

Solution:

We need to prove that $\frac{AG}{AD} = \frac{m_D}{m_G} = \frac{2}{3}$.

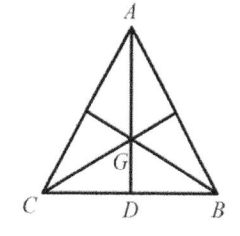

We label each line segment as shown.

Suppose that the mass at point C has a mass of 1, $m_C = 1$.
Since $BD = CD$, $m_B = m_C = 1$ and $m_D = m_B + m_C = 2$.

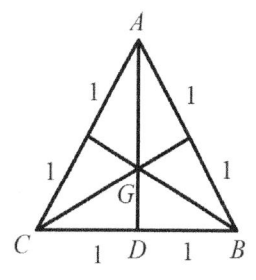

We know that $m_A = 1$. So $m_G = m_A + m_D = 3$.
$\frac{AG}{AD} = \frac{m_D}{m_G} = \frac{2}{3}$.

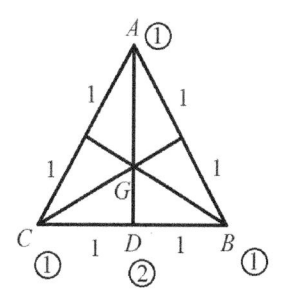

Example 9. In triangle ABC, AE bisects angle A and CD bisects angle C. The sides of triangle ABC are $AB = 5$, $AC = 4$ and $BC = 7$. Then $AF / FE = k (CF / FD)$ where k is:

(A) $\frac{45}{77}$ (B) $\frac{5}{7}$ (C) $\frac{7}{9}$ (D) $\frac{4}{7}$ (E) 1

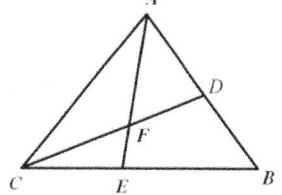

Solution: $\frac{45}{77}$.

By the Angle Bisector theorem, we have
$\frac{AC}{AB} = \frac{CE}{EB} = \frac{4}{5}$

27

The Mass Points Method **Chapter 2. Direct Application of Mass Points**

$$\frac{AC}{CB} = \frac{AD}{DB} = \frac{4}{7}$$

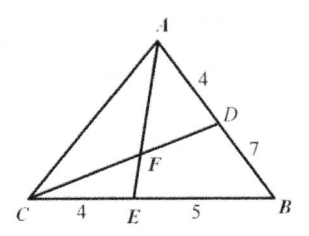

We label each line segment as shown.

We assign $m_B = 4$.
From the ratios we identified above, we find
$m_C = 5$, $m_E = 9$, and $m_A = 7$, $m_D = 11$.

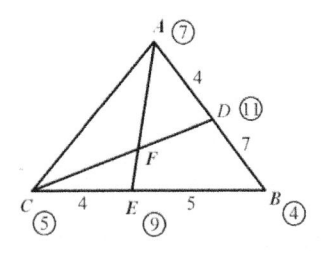

$$\frac{AF}{FE} = \frac{m_E}{m_A} = \frac{9}{7} \text{ and } \frac{CF}{FD} = \frac{m_D}{m_C} = \frac{11}{5}.$$

Thus we have $\frac{9}{7} = k\frac{11}{5} \quad \Rightarrow \quad k = \frac{45}{77}$.

Example 10. In triangle *ABC*, with $AB = AC = 3.6$, a point *D* is taken on *AB* at a distance 1.2 from *A*. Point *D* is joined to point *E* in the prolongation of *AC* so that triangle *AED* is equal in area to triangle *ABC*. Find the value of $DF : FE$.

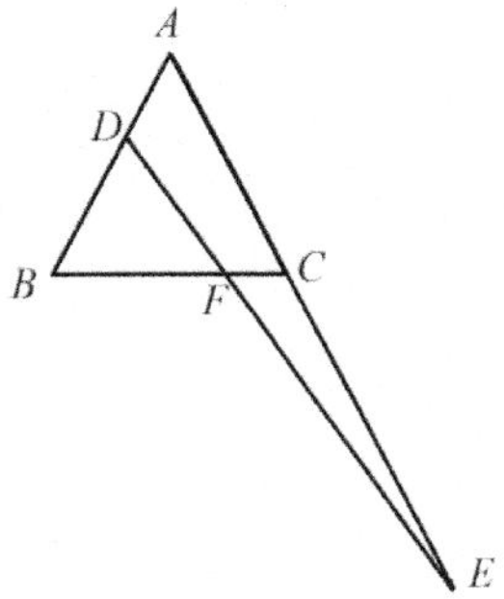

Solution: $\frac{1}{3}$.

$$\frac{DF}{FE} = \frac{m_E}{m_D}.$$

$AD : BD = 1.2 : (3.6 - 1.2) = 1 : 2$.

Since the triangle *AED* is equal in area to triangle *ABC*, we have $S_{\triangle ABC} = S_{\triangle ADE}$

$$\Rightarrow \quad \frac{1}{2} AB \times AC \sin \angle A = \frac{1}{2} AD \times AE \sin \angle A$$

$$\Rightarrow \quad \frac{1}{2} \times 3.6 \times 3.6 = \frac{1}{2} \times 1.2 \times AE \Rightarrow$$

$AE = 10.8$.

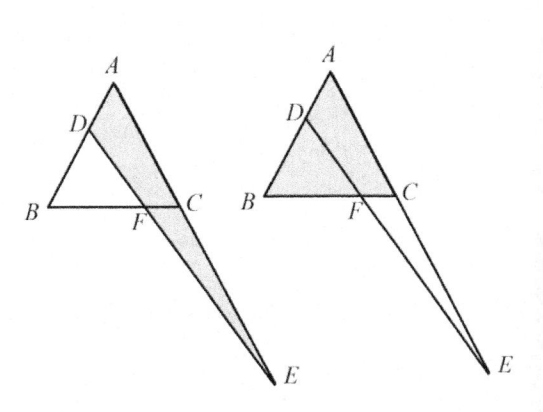

So $CE = AE - AC = 10.8 - 3.6 = 7.8 = 2AC$.

28

Now we label each line segment as shown.

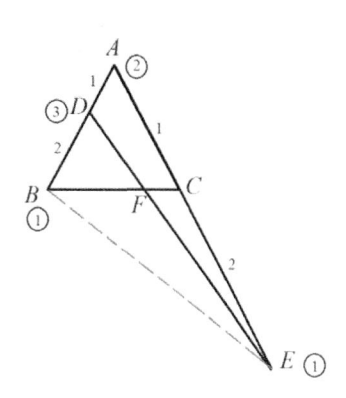

We assign $m_B = 1$. As a result, $m_A = 2$, $m_D = 3$, and $m_E = 1$.

This gives us
$$\frac{DF}{FE} = \frac{m_E}{m_D} = \frac{1}{3}.$$

Example 11. In triangle *ABC*, with $AB = AC = 3.6$, a point *D* is taken on *AB* at a distance 1.2 from *A*. Point D is joined to point *E* in the prolongation of *AC* so that triangle *AED* is equal in area to triangle *ABC*. Then $BF : FC$ equals:

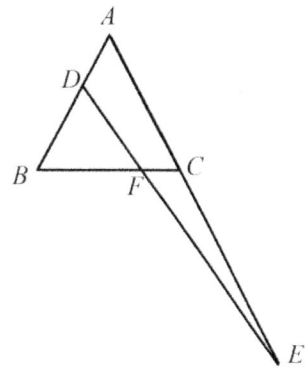

Solution: 3.
$$\frac{BF}{FC} = \frac{m_C}{m_B}.$$
$AD : BD = 1.2 : (3.6 - 1.2) = 1 : 2.$

Since the triangle *AED* is equal in area to triangle *ABC*, we have $S_{\triangle ABC} = S_{\triangle ADE}$

$\Rightarrow \quad \frac{1}{2} AB \times AC \sin \angle A = \frac{1}{2} AD \times AE \sin \angle A$

$\Rightarrow \quad \frac{1}{2} \times 3.6 \times 3.6 = \frac{1}{2} \times 1.2 \times AE \Rightarrow$

$AE = 10.8$.

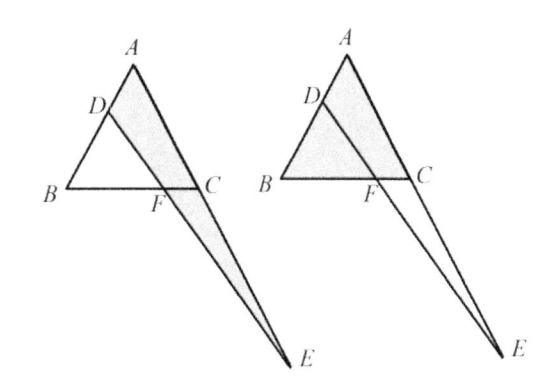

So $CE = AE - AC = 10.8 - 3.6 = 7.8 = 2AC$.

The Mass Points Method   **Chapter 2. Direct Application of Mass Points**

Next, we label each line segment as shown.
We assign $m_B = 1$.
As a result,
$m_A = 2$, $m_E = 1$, and $m_C = 3$.

$$\frac{BF}{FC} = \frac{m_C}{m_B} = \frac{3}{1} = 3.$$

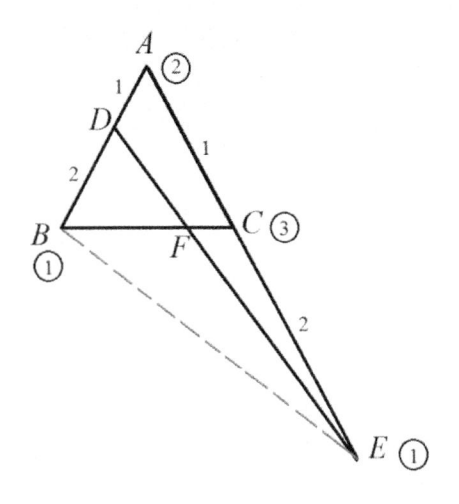

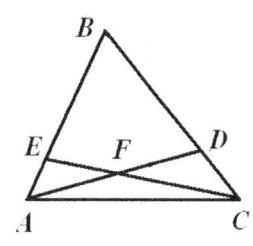

The Mass Points Method   Chapter 2. Direct Application of Mass Points

Chapter 2. Problems

Problem 1. (AMC) In triangle *ABC*, point *F* divides side *AC* in the ratio 1 : 2. Let *E* be the point of intersection of side *BC* and *AG* where *G* is the midpoint of *BF*. Then point *E* divides side *BC* in the ratio
(A) 1/4   (B) 1/3   (C) 2/5   (D) 4/11   (E) 3/8

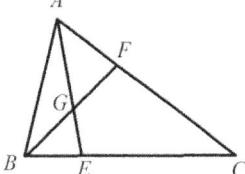

Problem 2. In $\triangle ABC$, points *D* and *E* lie on *BC* and *AB*, respectively. If *AD* and *CE* intersect at *G* so that $\dfrac{BD}{CD} = \dfrac{1}{3}$ and $\dfrac{AE}{BE} = \dfrac{1}{2}$, what is $\dfrac{AG}{DG}$? Express your answer as a common fraction.

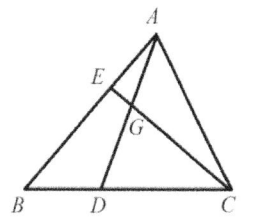

Problem 3. (AMC) Point *E* is selected on side *AB* of triangle *ABC* in such a way that *AE* : *EB* = 1 : 3 and point *D* is selected on side *BC* so that *CD* : *DB* = 1 : 2. The point of intersection of *AD* and *CE* is *F*. Then $\dfrac{EF}{FC} + \dfrac{AF}{FD}$ is
(A) $\dfrac{4}{5}$ (B) $\dfrac{5}{4}$ (C) $\dfrac{3}{2}$ (D) 2   (E) $\dfrac{5}{2}$

The Mass Points Method   **Chapter 2. Direct Application of Mass Points**

Problem 4. As shown in the figure, $\dfrac{AB}{BC} = \dfrac{DF}{FB} = 2$. Find $\dfrac{AF}{FE}$. Express your answer as a common fraction.

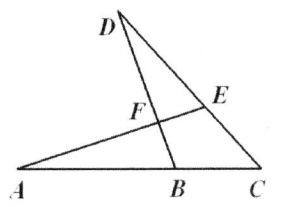

Problem 5. (AMC) In triangle ABC lines CE and AD are drawn so that $\dfrac{CD}{DB} = \dfrac{3}{1}$ and $\dfrac{AE}{EB} = \dfrac{3}{2}$. Let $r = \dfrac{CP}{PE}$, where P is the intersection point of CE and AD. Then r equals:

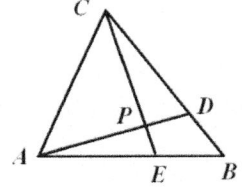

(A) 3 (B) $\dfrac{3}{2}$ (C) 4 (D) 5 (E) $\dfrac{5}{2}$

Problem 6. In $\triangle ABC$, points D, E and F lie on BC, AC and AB, respectively. If CF, AD, and BE intersect at G so that $\dfrac{CE}{EA} = \dfrac{1}{1}$ and $\dfrac{AF}{BF} = \dfrac{1}{3}$, what is $\dfrac{CD}{BD}$? Express your answer as a common fraction.

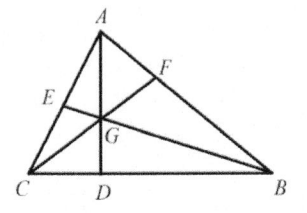

Problem 7. As shown in the figure, D is the midpoint of BC of $\triangle ABC$. Show that $AP = CP/2$ and $BE = 3EP$ if $DE = EA$.

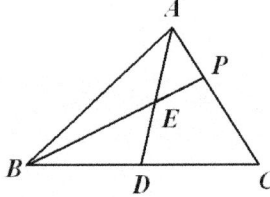

32

The Mass Points Method **Chapter 2. Direct Application of Mass Points**

Problem 8. *F* is the midpoint of *AB* of △*ABC*. *E* is on *AC* such that *AE* = 2/3 *AC*. Connect *BE* and *CF* to meet at *O*. Show that $OF = \frac{1}{2}CF$ and $OE = \frac{1}{4}BE$.

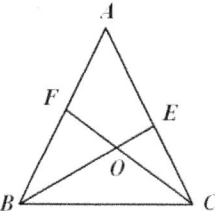

Problem 9. As shown in the figure, find $\frac{BF}{FC}$ if $\frac{AD}{DB} = \frac{5}{2}$ and $\frac{AC}{CE} = \frac{4}{3}$. Express your answer as a common fraction.

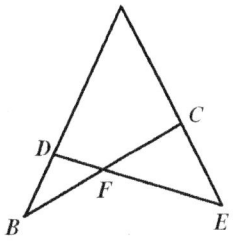

Problem 10. As shown in the figure, *ABC* is a triangle, *X* and *Y* are points on *BC* and *CA* respectively, and *R* is the point of intersection of *AX* and *BY*. Given *AY/YC* = *p*, and *AR/RX* = *q*, where 0 < *p* < *q*, express *BX/XC* in terms of *p* and *q*.

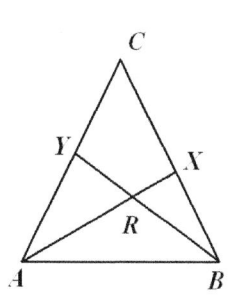

The Mass Points Method **Chapter 2. Direct Application of Mass Points**

Problem 11. Show that the cevians *AD*, *BE* and *CF* of △*ABC* are concurrent and $\dfrac{AF}{FB} \cdot \dfrac{BD}{DC} \cdot \dfrac{CE}{EA} = 1$.

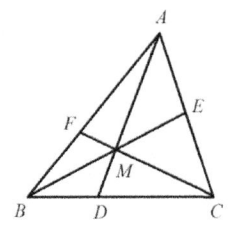

Problem 12. Point *E* is selected on side *AC* of triangle *ABC* in such a way that *AE* : *EC* = 3 : 4 and point *D* is selected on side *BC* so that *BD* : *DC* = 2 : 3. The point of intersection of *AD* and *BE* is *F*. Then $\dfrac{AF}{FD} \times \dfrac{BF}{FE}$ is

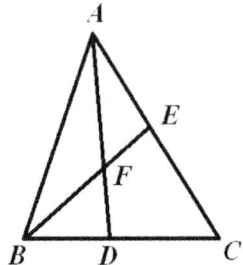

(A) $\dfrac{7}{3}$ (B) $\dfrac{14}{9}$ (C) $\dfrac{35}{12}$ (D) $\dfrac{56}{15}$ (E) $\dfrac{3}{1}$

Chapter 2. Solutions

Problem 1. Solution: (B).
Method 1 (Official Solution):
Draw *FH* parallel to line *AGE* (see figure). Then *BE* = *EH* because *BG* = *GF* and a line (*GE*) parallel to the base (*HF*) of a triangle (*HFB*) divides the other two sides proportionally.

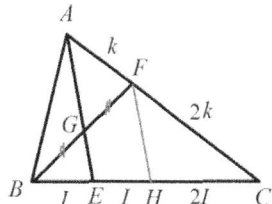

By the same reasoning applied to triangle *AEC* with line *FH* parallel to base *AE*, we see that *HC* = 2*EH*, because *FC* = 2*AF* is given. Therefore *EC* = *EH* + *HC* = 3*EH* = 3*BE*, and E divides side *BC* in the ratio 1: 3.

Method 2 (our solution):
Step 1: We label the length of each line segment as shown.

Step 2: Let the masses in each point be m_A, m_B, m_C, m_F and m_E, respectively.

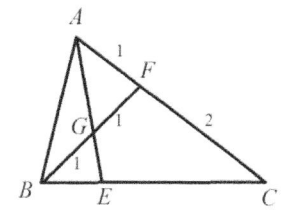

Step 3: We assign a mass of 1 to point *C*.

Note:

(1) This number can be randomly assigned. But it is better to choose the number such that (a) it is easy to compute other masses and (b) you avoid getting fractional values in your calculation.

(2) You can only assign one mass point a value. All others will be calculated based on the value using the seesaw formulas.

35

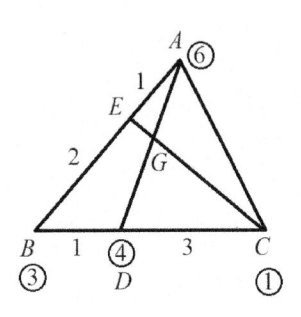

The Mass Points Method **Chapter 2. Direct Application of Mass Points**

Step 4: We set up equations and then solve.

Looking at the line segment AC, we have

$m_C \times 2 = m_A \times 1 \quad \Rightarrow \quad m_A = 2$.

$m_F = m_A + m_C = 2 + 1 = 3$.

Next, looking at the line segment BF, we have

$m_B \times 1 = m_F \times 1 \quad \Rightarrow \quad m_B = 3$.

So $\dfrac{BE}{EC} = \dfrac{1}{3}$.

Problem 2. Solution: $\dfrac{2}{3}$.

We label the length of each line segment as shown. Let the masses in each point be m_A, m_B, m_C, m_D, m_E, and m_G, respectively.

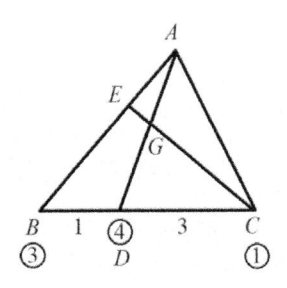

We assign a mass of 1 to point C.

$m_C \times 3 = m_B \times 1$

$\Rightarrow \quad m_B = 3$ and $m_D = m_B + m_C = 1 + 3 = 4$.

Next, we determine m_A.

$m_A \times 1 = m_B \times 2$

$\Rightarrow \quad m_A = 3 \times 2 = 6$

The last step is to find the answer:

$6 \times AG = 4 \times DG \quad \Rightarrow \quad \dfrac{AG}{DG} = \dfrac{4}{6} = \dfrac{2}{3}$.

Problem 3. Solution: (C).

Method 1 (Mass Points):
We label the length of each line segment as shown.

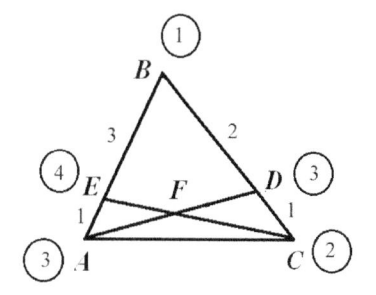

We assign a mass of 1 to point B.

Looking at the line segment BC:
$m_B \times 2 = m_C \times 1 \quad \Rightarrow \quad m_C = 2$ and
$m_D = m_B + m_C = 1 + 2 = 3$.

Looking at the line segment AB:
$m_A \times 1 = m_B \times 3 \Rightarrow \quad m_A = 3$.
$m_E = m_A + m_B = 3 + 1 = 4$.

Looking at the line segment CE:
$m_E \times EF = m_C \times FC$
$\Rightarrow \quad \dfrac{EF}{FC} = \dfrac{2}{4} = \dfrac{1}{2}$.

Looking at the line segment AD:
$m_A \times AF = m_D \times FD$
$\Rightarrow \quad \dfrac{AF}{FD} = \dfrac{3}{3} = 1$

Thus $(EF/FC) + (AF/FD) = \dfrac{1}{2} + 1 = \dfrac{3}{2}$.

Method 2:

Applying Menelaus' Theorem to $\triangle ECB$ with the transversal line FDA:

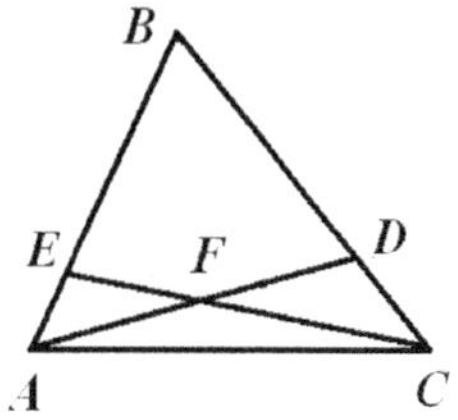

$\dfrac{EF}{CF} \cdot \dfrac{CD}{BD} \cdot \dfrac{AB}{EA} = 1$

$\Rightarrow \quad \dfrac{EF}{CF} \cdot \dfrac{1}{2} \cdot \dfrac{4}{1} = 1$

$\Rightarrow \quad \dfrac{EF}{CF} = \dfrac{1}{2}$ \hfill (1)

Applying Menelaus' Theorem to $\triangle ADB$ with the transversal line FCE:

$$\frac{AF}{DF} \cdot \frac{DC}{BC} \cdot \frac{BE}{AE} = 1 \quad \Rightarrow \quad \frac{AF}{DF} \cdot \frac{1}{3} \cdot \frac{3}{1} = 1$$

$$\Rightarrow \quad \frac{AF}{FD} = 1 \qquad\qquad (2)$$

(1) + (2): $\dfrac{EF}{CF} + \dfrac{AF}{FD} = \dfrac{1}{2} + 1 = \dfrac{3}{2}$.

Problem 4. Solution: $\dfrac{7}{2}$

Method 1:
We label the length of each line segment as shown.

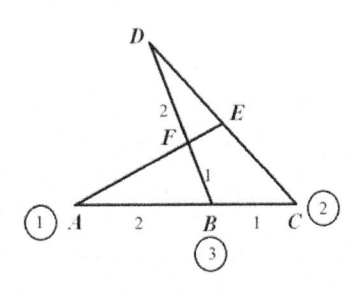

We assign a mass of 1 to point A.

$m_A \times 2 = m_C \times 1$

$\Rightarrow \quad m_C = 2$ and $m_B = m_A + m_C = 1 + 2 = 3$.

Similarly, $m_D \times 2 = m_B \times 3$

$\Rightarrow \quad m_D = \dfrac{3}{2}$.

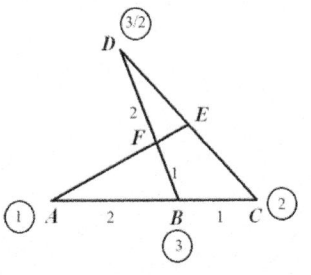

$m_E = m_D + m_C$
$= \dfrac{3}{2} + 2 = \dfrac{7}{2}$.

Taking a look at the line segment AE, we have

$m_A \times AF = m_E \times FE \quad \Rightarrow \quad \dfrac{AF}{FE} = \dfrac{\frac{7}{2}}{1} = \dfrac{7}{2}$.

Method 2:
Applying Menelaus' Theorem to $\triangle DBC$ with the transversal points F, A and E, we have

$$\frac{DF}{BF} \cdot \frac{BA}{CA} \cdot \frac{CE}{DE} = 1$$

$$\Rightarrow \quad \frac{DE}{CE} = \frac{DF}{BF} \cdot \frac{BA}{CA} = \frac{2}{1} \cdot \frac{2}{3} = \frac{4}{3}$$

Applying Menelaus' Theorem to $\triangle ACE$ with the transversal points B, D and F:

$$\frac{AB}{CB} \cdot \frac{CD}{ED} \cdot \frac{EF}{AF} = 1 \Rightarrow \frac{AF}{EF} = \frac{DC}{ED} \cdot \frac{AB}{CB} = \frac{7}{4} \cdot \frac{2}{1} = \frac{7}{2}$$

Problem 5. Solution: (D).

Method 1 (Mass Points):

We label the length of each line segment as shown.

We assign a mass of 3 to point B.

Looking at the line segment BC:

$m_B \times 1 = m_C \times 3$

$\Rightarrow \quad m_C = 1$.

Looking at the line segment AB:

$m_A \times 3 = m_B \times 2$

$\Rightarrow \quad m_A = 2$.

$m_E = m_A + m_B = 3 + 2 = 5$.

$\dfrac{CP}{PE} = \dfrac{5}{1} = 5$.

Method 2:

Applying Menelaus' Theorem to $\triangle BCE$ with the transversal points D, P, and A:

$$\frac{BD}{CD} \cdot \frac{CP}{EP} \cdot \frac{EA}{BA} = 1$$

$\Rightarrow \quad \dfrac{1}{3} \cdot r \cdot \dfrac{3}{5} = 1 \Rightarrow r = 5$.

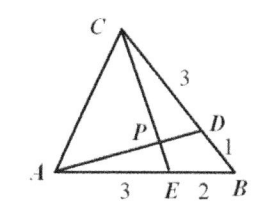

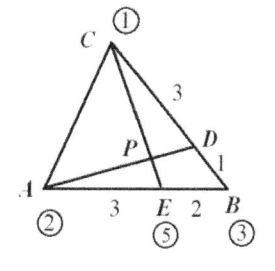

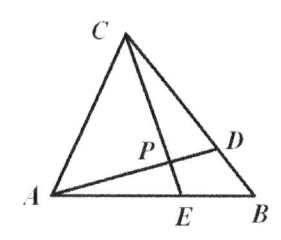

The Mass Points Method   Chapter 2. Direct Application of Mass Points

Problem 6. Solution: $\dfrac{1}{3}$.

We label the length of each line segment as shown.
Let the masses in each point be m_A, m_B, m_C, m_D, m_E, and m_G, respectively.

Let us assume that the figure balances on point G.

Suppose that the mass at point A has a mass of 3, $m_A = 3$.

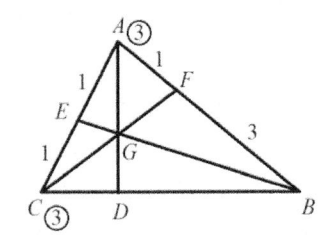

We have $m_C \times CE = m_A \times AE$.

We know that $AE = EC$. So $m_C = 3$.
Taking a look at the side AB, we have
$m_A \times AF = m_B \times BF$
$\Rightarrow \quad 3 \times 1 = m_B \times 3 \Rightarrow \quad m_B = 1$.

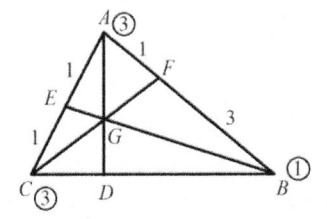

The final step is to find the answer:
$3 \times CD = 1 \times BD \quad \Rightarrow \quad \dfrac{CD}{BD} = \dfrac{1}{3}$.

Problem 7. Solution:
Method 1:
We label the length of each line segment as shown.
We assign a mass of 1 to point B.
$m_B \times 1 = m_C \times 1$
$\Rightarrow \quad m_C = 1$ and $m_D = m_B + m_C = 1 + 1 = 2$.

Since $DE = EA$, $m_A = m_D = 2$.

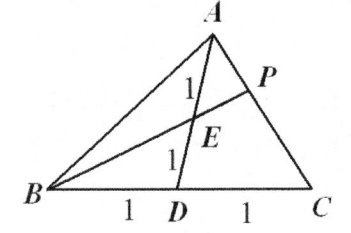

Now we look at the line segment AC:
$m_A \times AP = m_C \times CP \quad \Rightarrow \quad AP = \dfrac{CP}{2}$.

Thus, $m_P = m_A + m_C = 2 + 1 = 3$.

The Mass Points Method　　　Chapter 2. Direct Application of Mass Points

Now we look at the line segment *BP*:
$m_B \times BE = m_P \times EP \implies 1 \times BE = 3 \times EP$
$\implies BE = 3EP$.

Method 2:
Applying Menelaus' Theorem to $\triangle CDA$ with the transversal points *B*, *E* and *P*:
$$\frac{CB}{DB} \cdot \frac{DE}{AE} \cdot \frac{AP}{CP} = 1 \qquad (1)$$
We know that $BC = 2BD$, and $DE = EA$.
So (1) becomes: $\frac{2}{1} \cdot 1 \cdot \frac{AP}{CP} = 1 \implies AP = \frac{1}{2}CP$.

Applying Menelaus' Theorem to $\triangle CPB$ with the transversal points *A*, *E* and *D*:
$$\frac{CA}{PA} \cdot \frac{PE}{BE} \cdot \frac{BD}{CD} = 1 \qquad (2)$$
We know that $AC = 3AP$ and $BD = DC$, so (2) becomes: $BE = 3EP$.

Problem 8. Solution:
Method 1:
We label the length of each line segment as shown.
We assign a mass of 1 to point *B*.
$m_B \times 1 = m_A \times 1$
$\implies m_A = 1$ and $m_F = m_A + m_B = 1 + 1 = 2$.

Now we look at the line segment *AC*:
$m_A \times 2 = m_C \times 1 \implies m_C = 2$.
Thus, $m_E = m_A + m_C = 1 + 2 = 3$

Now we look at the line segment *CF*:
$m_C \times CO = m_F \times OF$

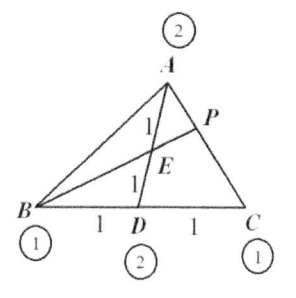

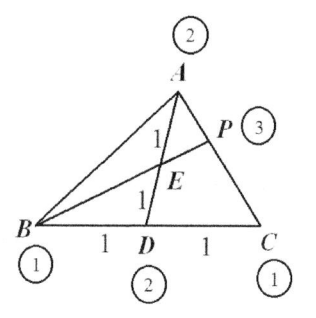

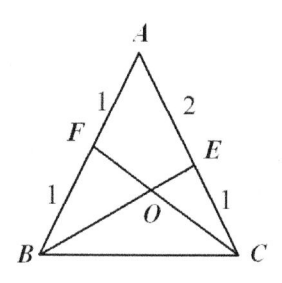

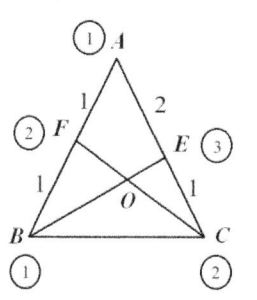

41

The Mass Points Method   Chapter 2. Direct Application of Mass Points

$\Rightarrow \quad 2 \times CO = 2 \times OF$
$\Rightarrow CO = OF$.
Then $OF = \dfrac{1}{2} CF$.

Similarly, we look at the line segment BE:
$m_B \times BO = m_E \times OE$
$\Rightarrow \quad 1 \times BO = 3 \times OE \quad\quad \Rightarrow BO = 3OE$.
We get $OE = \dfrac{1}{4} BE$.

Method 2:
Applying Menelaus' Theorem to triangle ACF with transversal points E, O, and B: 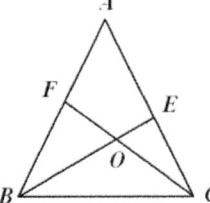
$\dfrac{AE}{EC} \cdot \dfrac{CO}{OF} \cdot \dfrac{FB}{BA} = 1 \quad \Rightarrow \quad \dfrac{2}{1} \cdot \dfrac{CO}{OF} \cdot \dfrac{1}{2} = 1$
$\therefore \ CO = OF, \quad \therefore \quad OF = \dfrac{1}{2} CF$.

Applying Menelaus' Theorem to triangle OBF with transversal points E, A, and C:
$\dfrac{OE}{BE} \cdot \dfrac{BA}{FA} \cdot \dfrac{FC}{OC} = 1 \quad \Rightarrow \quad \dfrac{OE}{BE} \cdot \dfrac{2}{1} \cdot \dfrac{2}{1} = 1$
$\Rightarrow \quad \dfrac{OE}{BE} = \dfrac{1}{4} \Rightarrow \ OE = \dfrac{1}{4} BE$.

Problem 9. Solution: 14/15.

Method 1:
We label the length of each line segment as shown.
We assign a mass of 6 to point A.

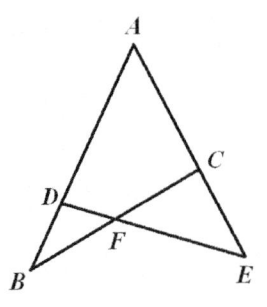

$m_A \times 5 = m_B \times 2$

$\Rightarrow \quad m_B = 15$.

Now we look at the line segment AE:
$m_A \times AC = m_E \times CE$

The Mass Points Method   **Chapter 2. Direct Application of Mass Points**

$\Rightarrow \quad m_E = 8$

$m_C = m_A + m_E = 16 + 8 = 14$.

Now we look at the line segment BC:

$m_B \times BF = m_C \times FC$

$\Rightarrow \quad \dfrac{BF}{FC} = \dfrac{14}{15}$.

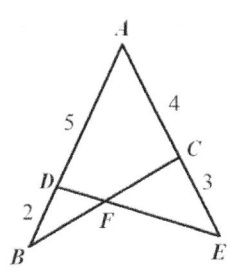

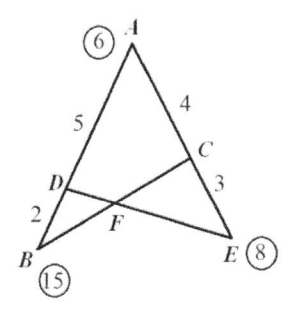

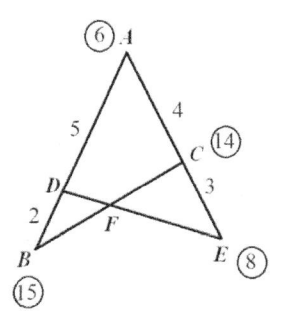

Method 2:
Applying Menelaus' Theorem to $\triangle ABC$ with the transversal DFE:

$\dfrac{AD}{DB} \cdot \dfrac{BF}{FC} \cdot \dfrac{CE}{EA} = 1$

We know that $\dfrac{AC}{CE} = \dfrac{4}{3}$, so $\dfrac{CE}{EA} = \dfrac{3}{7}$. We also know that

$\dfrac{AD}{DB} = \dfrac{5}{2}$.

$\therefore \dfrac{5}{2} \cdot \dfrac{BF}{FC} \cdot \dfrac{3}{7} = 1$, $\therefore \dfrac{BF}{FC} = \dfrac{14}{15}$.

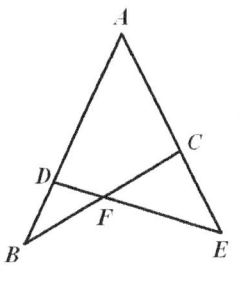

Problem 10. Solution: $\dfrac{p}{q-p}$.

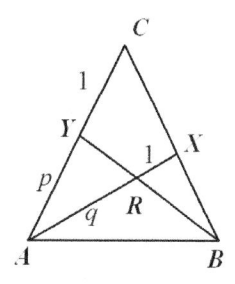

Method 1:
We label the length of each line segment as shown.
We assign a mass of 1 to point A.

43

$m_A \times p = m_C \times 1$

$\Rightarrow \quad m_C = p$.

Now we look at the line segment CB:

$m_A \times q = m_X \times 1 \quad \Rightarrow \quad m_X = q$

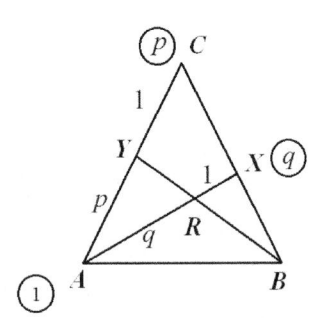

Now we look at the line segment BC:

$m_X = m_C + m_B = p + m_B \quad \Rightarrow \quad q = p + m_B$

$\Rightarrow \quad m_B = q - p$.

$\dfrac{BX}{XC} = \dfrac{m_C}{m_B} = \dfrac{p}{q-p}$.

Method 2:
Consider $\triangle AXC$ and its transversal BRY. By Menelaus' theorem,

$\dfrac{AR}{RX} \cdot \dfrac{XB}{BC} \cdot \dfrac{CY}{YA} = 1$.

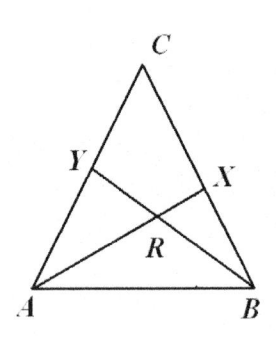

Thus $\dfrac{BC}{XB} = \dfrac{AR}{RX} \cdot \dfrac{CY}{YA} = \dfrac{q}{p}$, i.e., $\dfrac{BX + XC}{BX} = \dfrac{q}{p}$.

It follows that $1 + \dfrac{XC}{BX} = \dfrac{q}{p}$, $\dfrac{XC}{BX} = \dfrac{q}{p} - 1 = \dfrac{q-p}{p}$, i.e.,

$\dfrac{BX}{XC} = \dfrac{p}{q-p}$.

Problem 11. Proof:
Let the masses in each point be m_A, m_B, m_C, m_D, m_E, and m_G, respectively.

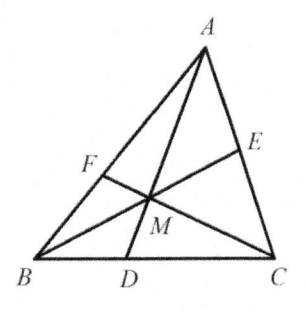

We pick the point E on AC such that

$\dfrac{CE}{EA} = \dfrac{m_A}{m_C} \quad\quad (1)$

The Mass Points Method   Chapter 2. Direct Application of Mass Points

By definition, E is the center of mass of AC. Therefore, the center of mass of points A, B, and C should be on the line segment of BE.
We also pick the point F on AB such that
$$\frac{AF}{FB} = \frac{m_B}{m_A} \qquad (2)$$
By definition, F is the center of mass of AB. Therefore, the center of mass of points A, B, and C should be on the line segment of CF.

It follows that the center of mass of points A, B, and C should be M, the point of intersection of the line segments CF and BE.

Similarly, we pick the point D on BC such that
$$\frac{BD}{DC} = \frac{m_C}{m_A} \qquad (3)$$

Since M is on AD, the lines AD, BE, and CF must all go through the point M. They are concurrent.

$(1) \times (2) \times (3)$:
$$\frac{CE}{EA} \times \frac{AF}{FB} \times \frac{BD}{DC} = \frac{m_A}{m_C} \times \frac{m_B}{m_A} \times \frac{m_C}{m_A} = 1.$$

Problem 12. Solution: (C).
Method 1 (the mass points method):
We label the length of each line segment as shown.

Let the masses in each point be m_A, m_B, m_C, m_D, m_E, and m_F, respectively.

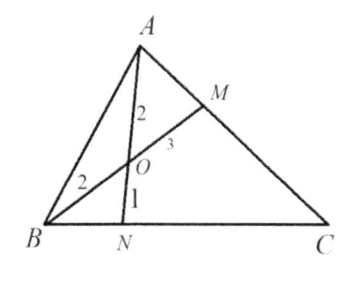

We assign a mass of 6 to point C.

45

It follows that $m_A = 8$, $m_E = 8 + 6 = 14$.
$m_B = 9$, $m_D = 9 + 6 = 15$.

Thus $\dfrac{AF}{FD} = \dfrac{15}{8}$ and $\dfrac{BF}{FE} = \dfrac{14}{9}$.

The answer is $\dfrac{AF}{FD} \times \dfrac{BF}{FE} = \dfrac{15}{8} \times \dfrac{14}{9} = \dfrac{35}{12}$.

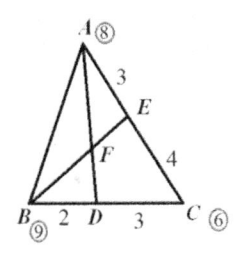

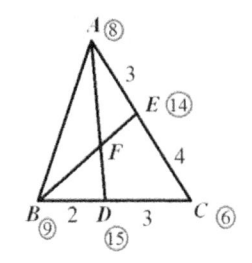

Method 2:
Draw $EG \parallel BC$ such that EG meets AD at G.

By similar triangles, $\dfrac{GE}{BD} = \dfrac{GE/DC}{BD/DC} = \dfrac{AE/AC}{BD/DC} = \dfrac{3/7}{2/3} = \dfrac{9}{14}$.

Therefore $\dfrac{FG}{DF} = \dfrac{FE}{BF} = \dfrac{GE}{BD} = \dfrac{9}{14}$.

We also have $\dfrac{DG}{DF} = \dfrac{23}{14}$, $\dfrac{AG}{AD} = \dfrac{3}{7}$, so $\dfrac{GD}{AD} = \dfrac{4}{7}$

$\Rightarrow GD = \dfrac{4}{7} AD$.

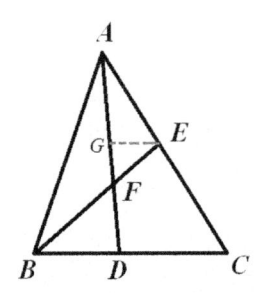

Thus $\dfrac{AD}{DF} = \dfrac{\frac{7}{4} GD}{DF} = \dfrac{7}{4} \cdot \dfrac{23}{14} = \dfrac{23}{8}$.

We also know that $\dfrac{AE}{DF} = \dfrac{15}{8}$.

Therefore $\dfrac{AF}{FD} \times \dfrac{BF}{FE} = \dfrac{15}{8} \times \dfrac{14}{9} = \dfrac{35}{12}$.

Chapter 3. Removing Line Segments

Example 1. As shown in the figure, D and E are points on BC of triangle ABC. The median BF meets AD and AE at G and H, respectively such that $BG : GH : HF = 5 : 3 : 2$. Find $\dfrac{BD}{BC}$.

Solution: $\dfrac{1}{3}$.

$\dfrac{BD}{BC} = \dfrac{m_C}{m_D}$

We remove the segment AE and label each line segment as shown.

We assign a mass of 1 to point C.

$m_A \times 1 = m_C \times 1 \Rightarrow \quad m_A = 1$.

$m_F = m_A + m_C = 1 + 1 = 2$.

$m_B \times 5 = m_F \times 5 \quad \Rightarrow \quad m_B = m_F = 2$.

$m_D = m_B + m_C = 2 + 1 = 3$

$\dfrac{BD}{BC} = \dfrac{m_C}{m_D} = \dfrac{1}{3}$.

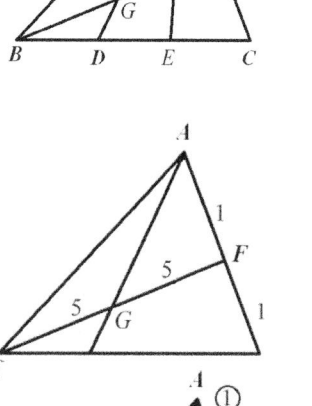

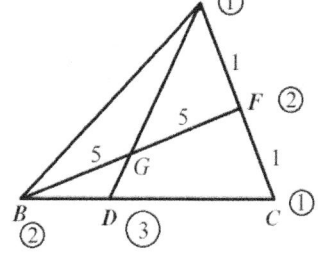

Example 2. For integers x, y and z, if $AB:BC = 1:3$, $AG:GH = 3:4$ and $AF:DF = 7:5$, then $EF:EB = x : y$ in simplest form. What is the value of $x + y$?

Solution: 14.

$\dfrac{EF}{EB} = \dfrac{m_B}{m_F}$.

We remove the segment AH.

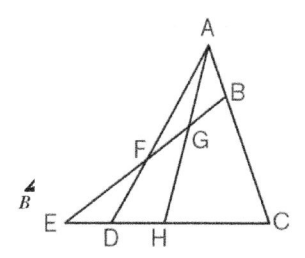

The Mass Points Method Chapter 3. Removing Line Segments

Then we label each line segment as shown.

We assign a mass of 25 to point C.

Taking a look at the side AC, we have:
$m_A \times 1 = m_C \times 3 \quad \Rightarrow \quad m_A = 75$.

Similarly, looking at the side AD, we have:
$m_A \times 7 = m_D \times 5 \Rightarrow \quad m_D = 105$.
$m_F = m_A + m_A = 105 + 75 = 180$

Finally, looking at the line segment CE:
$m_E = m_D - m_C = 105 - 25 = 80$
$\dfrac{EF}{EB} = \dfrac{m_B}{m_F} = \dfrac{100}{180} = \dfrac{5}{9}$.

The answer is $5 + 9 = 14$.

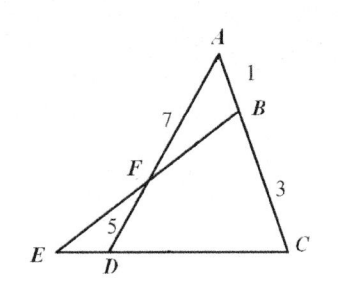

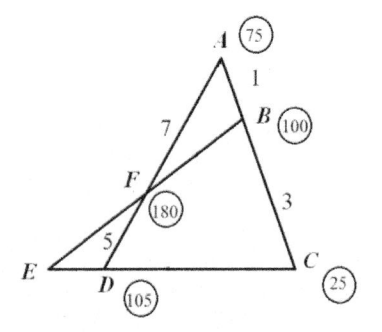

Example 3. As shown in the figure, D and E are points on BC of triangle ABC such that $BD : DE : EC = 1 : 1 : 1$. The median BF meets AD and AE at G and H respectively and is divided into the lengths of x, y, z ($x > y > z$). Find $x : y : z$.

Solution: $5 : 3 : 2$.

$\dfrac{x}{x+y+z} = \dfrac{BG}{BF} = \dfrac{m_F}{m_G}$.

$\dfrac{z}{x+y+z} = \dfrac{FH}{BF} = \dfrac{m_B}{m_H}$.

$\dfrac{y}{x+y+z} = 1 - \dfrac{x}{x+y+z} - \dfrac{y}{x+y+z}$.

We separate the original figure into two figures.

48

The Mass Points Method   Chapter 3. Removing Line Segments

The first figure is obtained by removing the segment AE, as shown on the right.

We know that H is the center of mass of A, B, and C, so E is the center of mass of B and C.

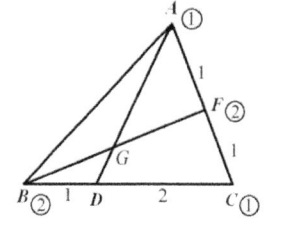

We assign a mass of 1 to point C.

$m_B \times 1 = m_C \times 2 \quad \Rightarrow \quad m_B = 2$.

F is the center of mass of A and C.

$m_A \times 1 = m_C \times 1 \Rightarrow \quad m_A = 1$.

It follows that $m_F = m_A + m_C = 1 + 1 = 2$.

$\dfrac{BG}{GF} = \dfrac{1}{1} \quad \Rightarrow \quad \dfrac{BG}{BF} = \dfrac{1}{2}$

$\Rightarrow \quad \dfrac{x}{x+y+z} = \dfrac{1}{2} \qquad (1)$

The second figure is obtained by removing the segment AD. Since H is the center of mass of A, B, and C, it follows that E is the center of mass of B and C and F is the center of mass of A and C.

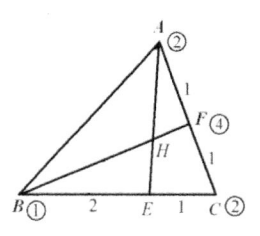

We assign a mass of 2 to point C.

$m_B \times 2 = m_C \times 1 \quad \Rightarrow \quad m_B = 1$.

$m_A \times 1 = m_C \times 1 \quad \Rightarrow \quad m_A = 2$.

Then $m_F = m_A + m_C = 2 + 2 = 4$.

$\dfrac{FH}{HB} = \dfrac{1}{4} \quad \Rightarrow \quad \dfrac{FH}{BF} = \dfrac{1}{5}$

$\Rightarrow \quad \dfrac{z}{x+y+z} = \dfrac{1}{5} \qquad (2)$

The Mass Points Method   **Chapter 3. Removing Line Segments**

Combining (1) and (2) gives us $\dfrac{y}{x+y+z} = 1 - \dfrac{1}{2} - \dfrac{1}{5} = \dfrac{3}{10}$.

It follows that $x : y : z = 5 : 3 : 2$.

Example 4. (Mathcounts) For integers x, y and z, if $AB:BC = 1:4$, $AG:GH = 3:5$ and $AF:DF = 5:4$, then $CH:DH:DE = x : y : z$. What is the value of $x + y + z$?

Solution: 60.

$$\dfrac{x}{x+y+z} = \dfrac{CH}{CE} = \dfrac{m_E}{m_H}.$$

$$\dfrac{z}{x+y+z} = \dfrac{ED}{CE} = \dfrac{m_C}{m_D}.$$

$$\dfrac{y}{x+y+z} = 1 - \dfrac{x}{x+y+z} - \dfrac{y}{x+y+z}.$$

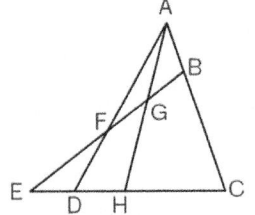

First figure is obtained by removing the segment AD.

We assign a mass of 5 to point C.

We look at the side AC.

$m_C \times 4 = m_A \times 1 \quad \Rightarrow \quad m_A = 20$.

Similarly, we look at the side AH.

$m_A \times 3 = m_H \times 5 \quad \Rightarrow \quad m_H = 12$.

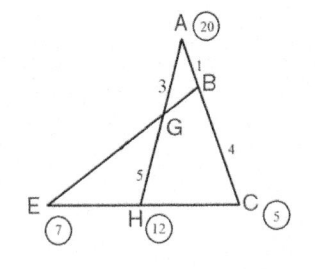

Now we look at the line segment CE: $m_H = m_E + m_C \Rightarrow m_E = 12 - 5 = 7$.

$$\dfrac{x}{x+y+z} = \dfrac{CH}{CE} = \dfrac{m_E}{m_H} = \dfrac{7}{12} = \dfrac{35}{60}.$$

Now we remove the segment AH.

We assign a mass of 5 to point D.

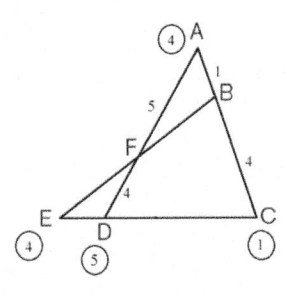

50

We look at the side *AD*.

$m_D \times 4 = m_A \times 5 \quad \Rightarrow \quad m_A = 4$.

Similarly, we look at the side *AC*.

$m_A \times 1 = m_C \times 4 \Rightarrow \quad m_C = 1$.

$$\frac{z}{x+y+z} = \frac{ED}{CE} = \frac{m_C}{m_D} = \frac{1}{5} = \frac{12}{60}.$$

So we know that $\dfrac{y}{x+y+z} = 1 - \dfrac{35}{60} - \dfrac{12}{60} = \dfrac{13}{60}$.

$x : y : z = 35 : 13 : 12$ and $x + y + z = 35 + 13 + 12 = 60$.

Example 5. As shown in the figure, *AD* is the angle bisector of $\angle A$ of triangle *ABC*. The perpendicular bisector of *AD* meets *AB* at *E*, *AC* at *G*, and the extension of *BC* at *F*. Find $\dfrac{CF}{BF}$ if $\dfrac{AC}{AB} = \dfrac{3}{4}$.

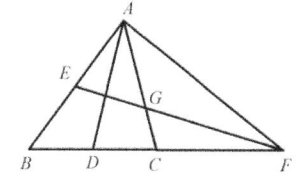

Solution: $\dfrac{9}{16}$.

Method 1:

$\dfrac{CF}{BF} = \dfrac{m_B}{m_C}$.

By the angle bisector theorem,

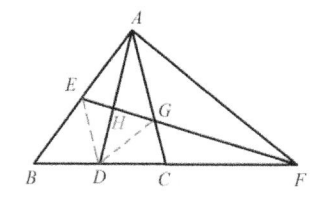

$\dfrac{AC}{AB} = \dfrac{CD}{DB} = \dfrac{3}{4}$.

We connect *DE* and *DG*.

Since *EG* is the perpendicular bisector of *AD*, *AEDG* is a parallelogram. So *DG* // *AB*, and *DE* // *AC*.

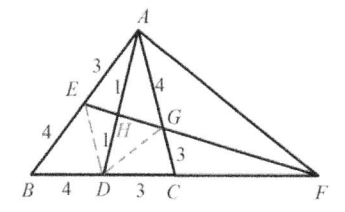

51

The Mass Points Method   **Chapter 3. Removing Line Segments**

Then we have
$$\frac{CD}{BD} = \frac{CG}{AG} = \frac{3}{4}$$

$$\frac{BD}{DC} = \frac{BE}{AE} = \frac{4}{3}$$

Now we remove the segment AD. We assign $m_B = 9$. And we get $m_A = 12$.

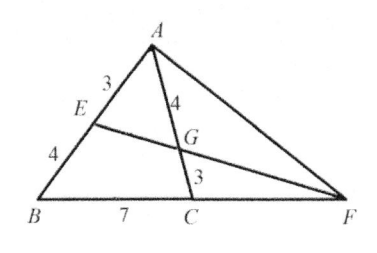

Then we get $m_A \times 4 = m_C \times 3$

$\Rightarrow m_C = 16$

$$\frac{CF}{BF} = \frac{m_B}{m_C} = \frac{9}{16}.$$

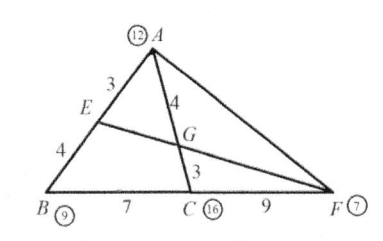

Method 2:
By the Angle Bisector theorem, we have
$$\frac{AC}{AB} = \frac{CD}{DB} = \frac{3}{4}.$$

Next, we connect DE and DG.

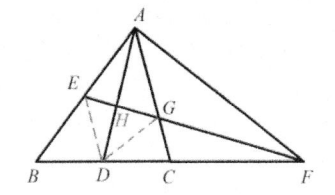

Since EG is the perpendicular bisector of AD, $AEDG$ is a parallelogram and so $DG \parallel AB$, and $DE \parallel AC$.

Then we have

$$\frac{CD}{BD} = \frac{CG}{AG} = \frac{3}{4}$$

$$\frac{BD}{DC} = \frac{BE}{AE} = \frac{4}{3}$$

Next we remove the segment AC and assign

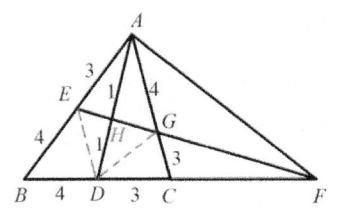

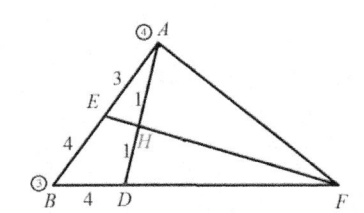

52

The Mass Points Method   **Chapter 3. Removing Line Segments**

$m_B = 3$. It follows that
$m_A = 4$, from which we can determine
$m_D = 4$ and $m_F = 1$.
We know that
$m_B \times 4 = m_F \times 1 \Rightarrow DF = 12$

$$\frac{CF}{BF} = \frac{DF - DC}{BF}$$

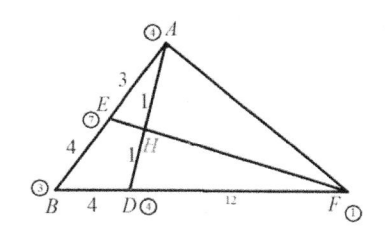

The answer is $\dfrac{CF}{BF} = \dfrac{12-3}{4+12} = \dfrac{9}{16}$.

The Mass Points Method   Chapter 3. Removing Line Segments

Chapter 3. Problems

Problem 1 As shown in the figure, D and E are points on BC of triangle ABC. The median BF meets AD and AE at G and H, respectively such that $BG : GH : HF = 5 : 3 : 2$. Find $\dfrac{AG}{AD}$.

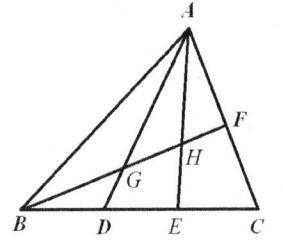

Problem 2. For integers x, y and z, if $AB:BC = 1:3$, $AG:GH = 3:4$ and $AF:DF = 7:5$, then $ED:DC = x : y$ in simplest form. What is the value of $x + y$?

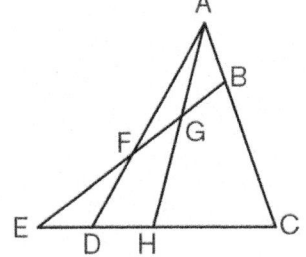

Problem 3. As shown in the figure, in $\triangle ABC$, $AG = \dfrac{1}{3} AB$, $BE = \dfrac{1}{3} BC$, $CF = \dfrac{1}{3} CA$. Find $AN : NL : LE$.

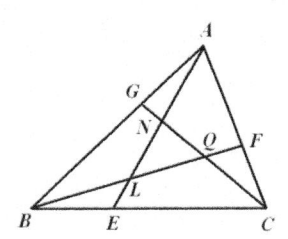

The Mass Points Method **Chapter 3. Removing Line Segments**

Problem 4. As shown in the figure, E and F are points on BC of triangle ABC such that $BE:EF:FC = 1:2:3$. The median BD meets AE and AF at M and N respectively and is divided into the lengths of x, y, z. Find $x:y:z$.

Problem 5. As shown in the figure, P and Q are points on AC of triangle ABC such that $AP:PQ:QC = 1:2:3$. The line segment AR meets BP and BQ at D and E respectively and divided BC into the ratio of $1:2$. Find $\dfrac{S_{PQED}}{S_{\triangle ABC}}$.

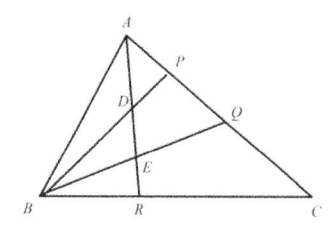

The Mass Points Method   **Chapter 3. Removing Line Segments**

Chapter 3. Solutions

Problem 1. Solution: $\dfrac{3}{4}$.

$$\dfrac{AG}{AD} = \dfrac{m_D}{m_G}$$

We remove the segment AE and label each line segment as shown.

We assign a mass of 1 to point C.
$m_A \times 1 = m_C \times 1 \Rightarrow \quad m_A = 1$.

$m_F = m_A + m_C = 1 + 1 = 2$.

$m_B \times 5 = m_F \times 5 \quad \Rightarrow \quad m_B = m_F = 2$.

$m_D = m_B + m_C = 2 + 1 = 3$

$m_G = m_B + m_F = 2 + 2 = 4$

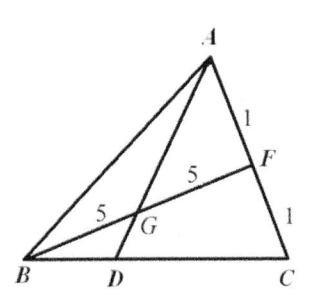

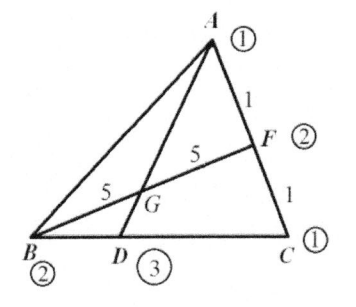

$\dfrac{AG}{GD} = \dfrac{m_D}{m_G} = \dfrac{3}{4}$.

Problem 2. Solution: 21.

$\dfrac{ED}{DC} = \dfrac{m_C}{m_D}$.

We remove the segment AH and label each line segment as shown.

We assign a mass of 25 to point C.

We look at the side AC.
$m_A \times 1 = m_C \times 3 \quad \Rightarrow \quad m_A = 75$.

Similarly, we look at the side AD.

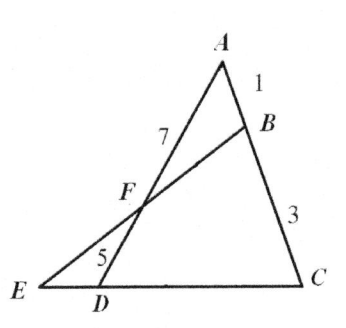

The Mass Points Method   **Chapter 3. Removing Line Segments**

$m_A \times 7 = m_D \times 5 \Rightarrow m_D = 105$.

$m_F = m_A + m_A = 105 + 75 = 180$

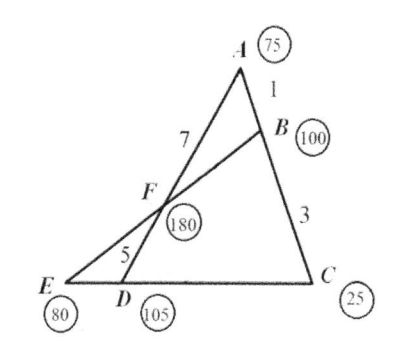

Now we look at the line segment *CE*:
$m_E = m_D - m_C = 105 - 25 = 80$

$\dfrac{ED}{DC} = \dfrac{m_C}{m_D} = \dfrac{25}{80} = \dfrac{5}{16}$.

The answer is 5 + 16 = 21.

Problem 3. Solution: 3 : 3 : 1.
Method 1 (Mass Points):
We separate the original figure into two figures.
The first figure is obtained by removing the segment *BF*.
We label the length of each line segment as shown.
We assign a mass of 2 to point *B*.

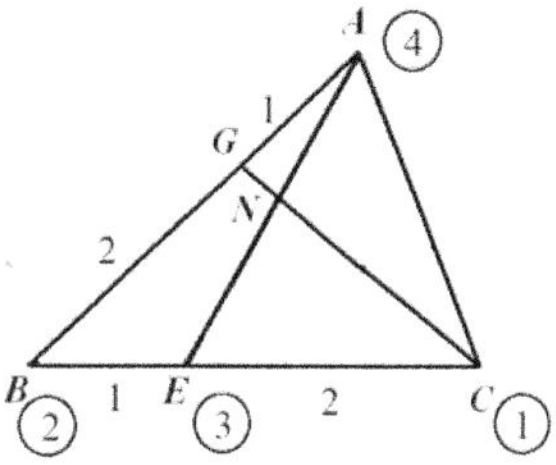

$m_B \times 1 = m_C \times 2$

$\Rightarrow m_C = 1$.

$m_E = m_B + m_C = 2 + 1 = 3$.

Now we look at the line segment *AB*:
$m_A \times 1 = m_B \times 3 \Rightarrow m_A = 4$.

Now we look at the line segment *AE*:
$m_A \times AN = m_E \times EN \Rightarrow \dfrac{AN}{EN} = \dfrac{3}{4}$

$\Rightarrow \dfrac{AN}{AE} = \dfrac{3}{7}$.

The second figure is obtained by removing the segment *CG*.
We label the length of each line segment as shown.

57

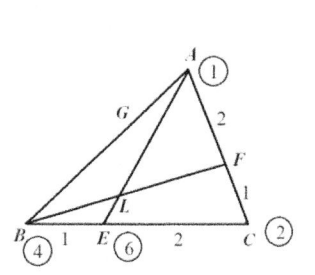

The Mass Points Method   Chapter 3. Removing Line Segments

We assign a mass of 2 to point C.

$m_B \times 1 = m_C \times 2 \quad \Rightarrow \quad m_B = 4$.

$m_E = m_B + m_C = 2 + 4 = 6$.

Now we look at the line segment AC:
$m_A \times 2 = m_C \times 1 \Rightarrow m_A = 1$.

Now we look at the line segment AE: $m_E \times LE = m_A \times AL \Rightarrow \dfrac{LE}{AL} = \dfrac{1}{6} \Rightarrow \dfrac{LE}{AE} = \dfrac{1}{7}$.

$\dfrac{NL}{AE} = 1 - \dfrac{AN}{AE} - \dfrac{LE}{AE} = 1 - \dfrac{3}{7} - \dfrac{1}{7} = \dfrac{3}{7}$.

$AN: NL: LE = \dfrac{3}{7} : \dfrac{3}{7} : \dfrac{1}{7} = 3 : 3 : 1$.

Method 2:
Let $AN = x$, $NL = y$, $LE = z$.

Applying Menelaus' Theorem to $\triangle AEB$ with the transversal points N, C, and G:

$\dfrac{AN}{EN} \cdot \dfrac{EC}{BC} \cdot \dfrac{BG}{AG} = 1$, or $\dfrac{x}{y+z} \cdot \dfrac{2}{3} \cdot \dfrac{2}{1} = 1$

$\Rightarrow \quad 4x = 3y + 3z \quad\quad\quad (1)$

Applying Menelaus' Theorem to $\triangle AEC$ with the transversal points L, B, and F:

$\dfrac{AL}{EL} \cdot \dfrac{EB}{CB} \cdot \dfrac{CF}{AF} = 1$, or $\dfrac{x+y}{z} \cdot \dfrac{1}{3} \cdot \dfrac{1}{2} = 1$

$\Rightarrow \quad x + y = 6z \quad\quad\quad (2)$

Solving (1) and (2) gives us: $x = y = 3z$.
$AN: NL: LE = 3 : 3 : 1$.

The Mass Points Method **Chapter 3. Removing Line Segments**

Problem 4. Solution: 6 : 8 : 7.

We separate the original figure into two figures.

The first figure is obtained by removing the segment *AF*.

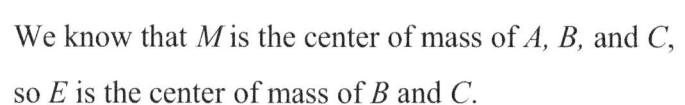

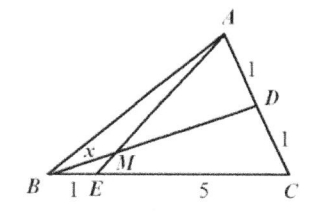

We know that *M* is the center of mass of *A*, *B*, and *C*, so *E* is the center of mass of *B* and *C*.

We assign a mass of 1 to point *C*.

$m_B \times 1 = m_C \times 5$

$\Rightarrow \quad m_B = 5$.

Since $AD = CD$, $m_A = 1$.

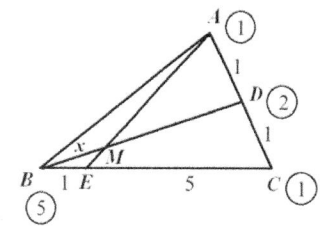

$\dfrac{BM}{DM} = \dfrac{2}{5} \quad \Rightarrow \quad \dfrac{BM}{BD} = \dfrac{2}{7}$

$\Rightarrow \quad \dfrac{x}{x+y+z} = \dfrac{2}{7} = \dfrac{6}{21}$ \quad (1)

The second figure is obtained by removing the segment *AE*.

We know that *N* is the center of mass of *A*, *B*, and *C*, so *D* is the center of mass of *A* and *C* and *F* is the center of mass of *B* and *C*.

If we assign a mass of 1 to point *C*, we get

$m_B = 1$, $m_A = 1$, and $m_D = 2$.

$\dfrac{ND}{NB} = \dfrac{1}{2} \quad \Rightarrow \quad \dfrac{ND}{BD} = \dfrac{1}{3}$

$\Rightarrow \quad \dfrac{z}{x+y+z} = \dfrac{1}{3} = \dfrac{7}{21}$ \quad (2)

So we know that $\dfrac{y}{x+y+z} = 1 - \dfrac{2}{7} - \dfrac{1}{3} = \dfrac{8}{21}$.

$x : y : z = 6 : 8 : 7$.

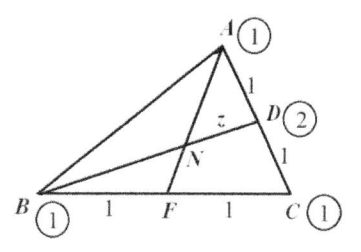

The Mass Points Method **Chapter 3. Removing Line Segments**

Method 2:
Applying Menelaus' Theorem to $\triangle BCD$ with the transversal points E, A, and M:
$$\frac{BE}{CE} \cdot \frac{CA}{DA} \cdot \frac{DM}{BM} = 1, \text{ or } \frac{1}{5} \cdot \frac{2}{1} \cdot \frac{y+z}{x} = 1$$
$\Rightarrow \quad 5x = 2y + 2z \qquad (1)$

Applying Menelaus' Theorem to $\triangle BCD$ with the transversal points F, A, and N:
$$\frac{BF}{CF} \cdot \frac{CA}{DA} \cdot \frac{DN}{BN} = 1, \text{ or } \frac{3}{3} \cdot \frac{2}{1} \cdot \frac{z}{x+y} = 1$$
$\Rightarrow \quad 2z = x + y \qquad (2)$

Solving (1) and (2) gives us:
$x : y = 3 : 4$ and $y : z = 8 : 7$.
Therefore $x : y : z = 6 : 8 : 7$.

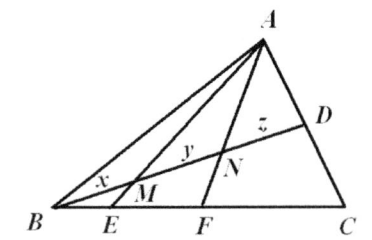

Problem 5. Solution: $\dfrac{5}{24}$.

We separate the original figure into two figures.

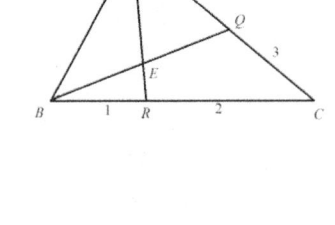

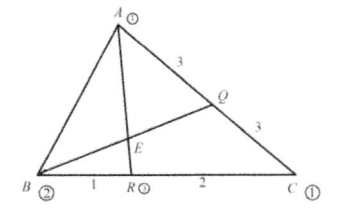

The first figure is obtained by removing the segment BP.

We assign a mass of 1 to point C.

$m_B \times 1 = m_C \times 2$

$\Rightarrow \quad m_B = 2$.

It follows that $m_A = 1$.

Thus $m_R = 1 + 2 = 3$.

$\dfrac{AE}{AR} = \dfrac{3}{4} = \dfrac{6}{8}$.

The Mass Points Method   **Chapter 3. Removing Line Segments**

The second figure is obtained by removing the segment BQ.

We assign a mass of 1 to point C.

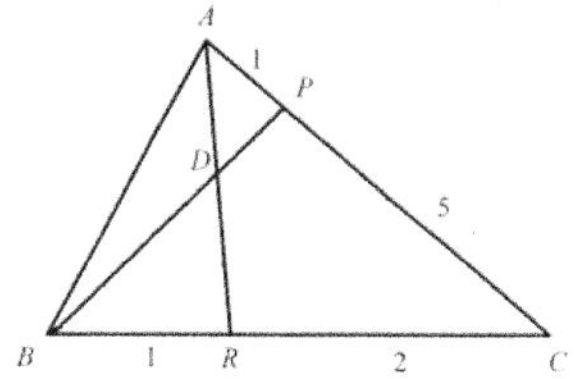

$m_B \times 1 = m_C \times 2$

$\Rightarrow \quad m_B = 2$.

It follows that $m_A = 5$.

Thus $m_R = 1 + 2 = 3$.

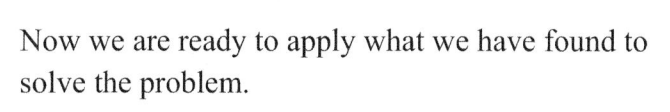

$\dfrac{AD}{AR} = \dfrac{3}{8}$.

$\dfrac{DE}{AR} = \dfrac{6}{8} - \dfrac{3}{8} = \dfrac{3}{8}$.

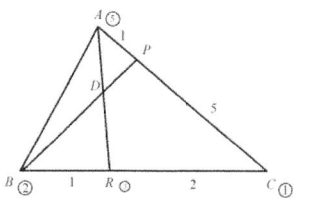

Now we are ready to apply what we have found to solve the problem.

Let the area of triangle ABC be 60.

It follows that the area of triangle ABR is 20, the area of triangle ARC is 40, and the area of triangle PBQ is one third of 60, or 20.

Since $\dfrac{DE}{AR} = \dfrac{3}{8}$, $\dfrac{S_{\triangle BDF}}{S_{\triangle ABR}} = \dfrac{3}{8}$

$\Rightarrow S_{\triangle BDF} = \dfrac{3}{8} \times 20 = \dfrac{15}{2}$.

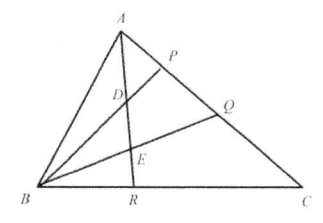

$\dfrac{S_{PQED}}{S_{\triangle ABC}} = \dfrac{S_{APBQ} - S_{\triangle BDF}}{S_{\triangle ABC}} = \dfrac{20 - \dfrac{15}{2}}{60} = \dfrac{5}{24}$.

The Mass Points Method — Chapter 4. Splitting Mass Points

Chapter 4. Splitting Mass Points

Example 1. In triangle ABC, points D, E, and F are on BC, AC, and AB respectively. If $BD : DC = 1$, $AE : EC = 1/3$, and $AF : FB = 1/2$. Line segment EF hits AD at point P. Find the ratio $AP : PD$. Express your answer as a common fraction.

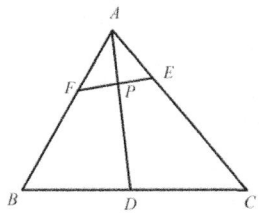

Solution: $\dfrac{2}{5}$.

We will use a technique called "splitting mass" to help us handle the transversal EF.

Let the masses in each point be m_A, m_B, m_C, and m_D, respectively.

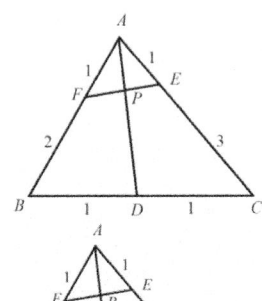

We assign a mass of 1 to point B.

$m_C \times 1 = m_B \times 1$

$\Rightarrow \quad m_C = 1$ and $m_D = m_B + m_C = 1 + 1 = 2$.

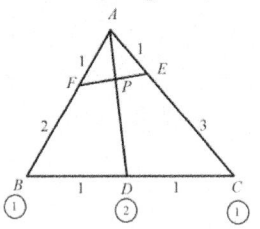

Now we determine m_A by splitting masses.

We look at the side AB and apply the mass points method to line AB, using $m_{A_{AB}}$ and m_B, with F as the center of mass.

$m_{A_{AB}} \times 1 = m_B \times 2$

$\Rightarrow \quad m_{A_{AB}} = 2$

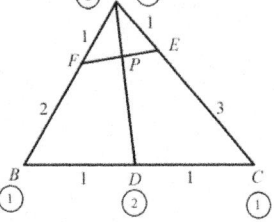

We look at the side AC and apply the mass points method to line AC, using $m_{A_{AC}}$ and m_C, with E the center of mass.

$m_{A_{AC}} \times 1 = m_C \times 3 \qquad \Rightarrow \qquad m_{A_{AC}} = 3$.

The Mass Points Method **Chapter 4. Splitting Mass Points**

Thus, $m_A = m_{A_{AB}} + m_{A_{AC}} = 2 + 5 = 5$

Finally, we apply the mass points method to line AD, using m_A and m_D to get the answer:

$m_A \times AP = m_D \times PD \quad \Rightarrow \quad \dfrac{AP}{PD} = \dfrac{2}{5}.$

Example 2. In triangle ABC, ED joins points E and D on the sides of AB and BC, respectively forming a transversal with $AE : BE = 4 : 3$, and $BD : CD = 5 : 2$. BG divides AC in a ratio of 3 to 7, and intersects ED at point F. Find the ratio $EF : FD$. Express your answer as a common fraction.

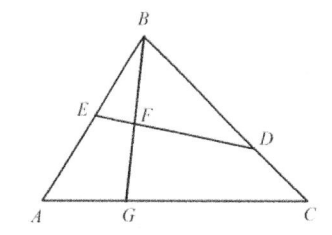

Solution: $\dfrac{9}{35}$.

(1) We label the length of each line segment as shown.

Let the masses in each point be m_A, m_B, m_C, and m_D, respectively. In order to find the ratio $EF : FD$, we need to find m_E and m_D.

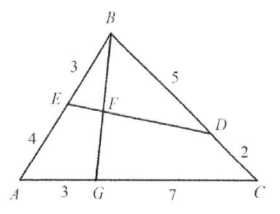

(2) We assign a mass of 105 to point A.

Taking a look at the side BC, we have

$m_C \times 7 = m_A \times 3$

$\Rightarrow \quad m_C = 45.$

We can determine m_B by splitting masses.

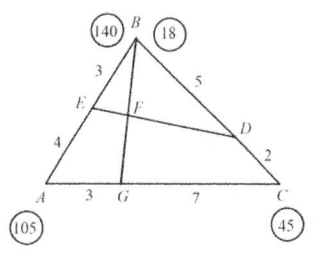

We look at side AB, and apply the mass points method to line AB, using $m_{A_{AB}}$ and m_B, with E as the center of mass.

$m_{B_{AB}} \times 3 = m_A \times 4$

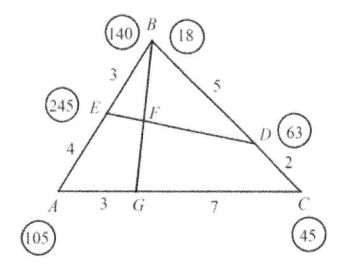

63

The Mass Points Method Chapter 4. Splitting Mass Points

$\Rightarrow \quad m_{B_{AB}} = 140$

$m_E = m_A + m_B = 105 + 140 = 245$.

We look at the side BC and apply the mass points method to line BC with D as the center of mass.

$m_{B_{BC}} \times 5 = m_C \times 2$

$\Rightarrow \quad m_{B_{BC}} = 18$.

Thus $m_B = m_{B_{AB}} + m_{B_{BC}} = 140 + 18 = 158$

$m_D = m_C + m_B = 45 + 18 = 63$

Finally, we look at the side ED and apply the mass points method to line ED with F as the center of mass to find the answer:

$m_E \times EF = m_D \times FD \quad \Rightarrow \quad \dfrac{EF}{FD} = \dfrac{63}{245} = \dfrac{9}{35}$.

Example 3. (Mathcounts) Triangle ABC, shown here, has cevian AD and transversal EF intersecting at G, with $AE : CE = 1 : 2$, $AF : BF = 5 : 4$ and $BD : CD = 3 : 2$. What is the ratio of AG to DG? Express your answer as a common fraction.

Solution: 25/38.

(1) We label the length of each line segment as shown.

Let the masses in each point be m_A, m_B, m_C, and m_D, respectively. In order to find the ratio of AG to DG, we need to find m_A and m_D.

(2) We assign a mass of 10 to point B.

Now we can determine m_A by splitting masses.

We look at the side AB, and apply the mass points method to line AB, using $m_{A_{AB}}$ and m_B with F as the center of

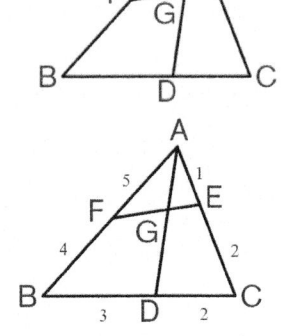

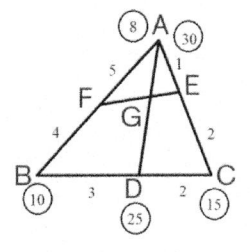

The Mass Points Method   Chapter 4. Splitting Mass Points

mass.
$$m_B \times 4 = m_{A_{AB}} \times 5 \quad \Rightarrow \quad m_{A_{AB}} = 8.$$

We look at the side BC and apply the mass points method to line BC with D as the center of mass.
$$m_B \times 3 = m_C \times 2$$
$$\Rightarrow m_C = 15.$$
$$m_D = m_B + m_C = 10 + 15 = 25.$$

We look at the side AC and apply the mass points method to line AC, using $m_{A_{AC}}$ and m_C, with E the center of mass.
$$m_{A_{AC}} \times 1 = m_C \times 2$$
$$\Rightarrow \quad m_{A_{AC}} = 30$$
$$m_A = m_{A_{AB}} + m_{A_{AC}} = 8 + 30 = 38.$$

Finally, we look at the side AD, with G as the center of mass, and get the answer:
$$m_A \times AG = m_D \times DG \quad \Rightarrow \quad \frac{AG}{DG} = \frac{m_D}{m_A} = \frac{25}{38}.$$

Example 4. (AMC) In triangle ABC shown in the adjoining figure, M is the midpoint of side BC, $AB = 12$ and $AC = 16$. Points E and F are taken on AC and AB, respectively, and lines EF and AM intersect at G.
If $AE = 2AF$ then EG/GF equals
(A) 3/2   (B) 4/3   (C) 5/4   (D) 6/5
(E) not enough information given to solve the problem

Solution: A.
We use a different method from the official solution to solve this problem.

65

The Mass Points Method Chapter 4. Splitting Mass Points

Let $AF = n$. We label the length of each line segment as shown.

Let the masses in each point be m_A, m_B, m_C, m_E, m_F, and m_M, respectively. In order to find EG/GF, we need to find m_F and m_E.

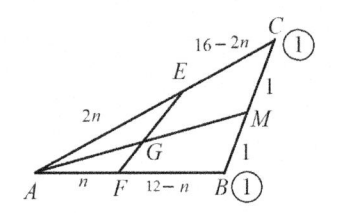

We assign a mass of 1 to point B.
Since $BM = CM$, $m_C = 1$.

Now we can determine m_A by splitting masses.
We look at the side AB, and apply the mass points method to line AB, using $m_{A_{AB}}$ and m_B with F as the center of mass.

$$m_B \times (12-n) = m_{A_{AB}} \times n \implies m_{A_{AB}} = \frac{12-n}{n}.$$

We look at the side AC and apply the mass points method to line AC, using $m_{A_{AC}}$ and m_C, with E the center of mass

$$m_{A_{AC}} \times 2n = m_C \times (16-n)$$

$$\implies m_{A_{AC}} = \frac{16-2n}{2n} = \frac{8-n}{n}.$$

$$m_E = m_{A_{AC}} + m_C = \frac{8-n}{n} + 1 = \frac{8}{n}.$$

$$m_F = m_{A_{AB}} + m_B = \frac{12-n}{n} + 1 = \frac{12}{n}.$$

Finally, we look at the side EF, with G as the center of mass to get the answer:
$m_E \times EG = m_F \times GF$

$$\implies \frac{EG}{GF} = \frac{m_F}{m_G} = \frac{\frac{12}{n}}{\frac{8}{n}} = \frac{12}{8} = \frac{3}{2}.$$

The Mass Points Method   **Chapter 4. Splitting Mass Points**

Example 5. As shown in the figure, *AM* is the median of $\triangle ABC$. Line segment *PQ* meets *AB* at *P*, *AC* at *Q*, and *AM* at *N*. Show $\dfrac{AC}{AQ} + \dfrac{AB}{AP} = \dfrac{2AM}{AN}$.

Proof:
Method 1:
We assign $m_B = 1$, giving us $m_C = 1$ and $m_M = 2$.

$$\frac{AB}{AP} = \frac{m_P}{m_B} = \frac{m_P}{1} = m_P \qquad (1)$$

$$\frac{AC}{AQ} = \frac{m_Q}{m_C} = \frac{m_Q}{1} = m_Q \qquad (2)$$

$$\frac{AM}{AN} = \frac{m_N}{m_M} = \frac{m_N}{2} \qquad (3)$$

We also know that $m_P + m_Q = m_N$ (4)

Substituting (1), (2), and (3) into (4):

$$\frac{AB}{AP} + \frac{AC}{AQ} = \frac{2AM}{AN}.$$

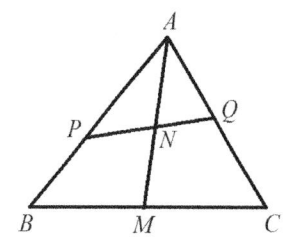

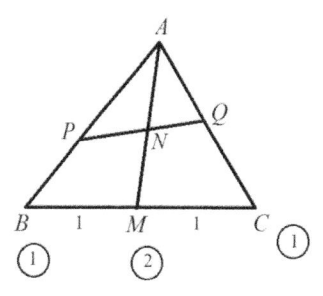

Method 2:

Since $BM = CM$, $S_{\triangle ABM} = S_{\triangle ACM} = \dfrac{S_{\triangle ABC}}{2}$

For $\triangle APN$ and $\triangle ABM$, we have

$$\frac{S_{\triangle APN}}{S_{\triangle ABM}} = \frac{AP \times AN}{AB \times AM} \qquad (1)$$

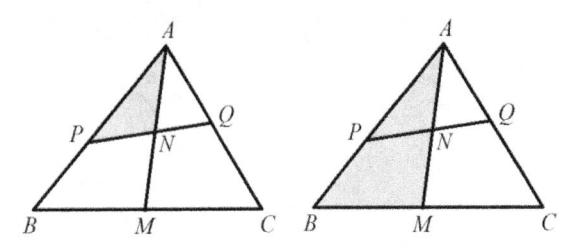

For $\triangle AQN$ and $\triangle ACM$, we have

$$\frac{S_{\triangle AQN}}{S_{\triangle ACM}} = \frac{AQ \times AN}{AC \times AM} \qquad (2)$$

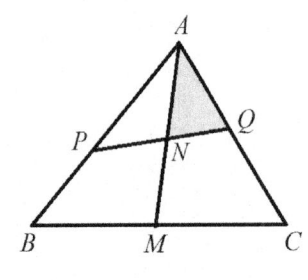

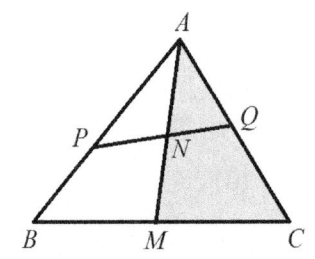

For $\triangle APQ$ and $\triangle ABC$, we have

$$\frac{S_{\triangle APQ}}{S_{\triangle ABC}} = \frac{AP \times AQ}{AB \times AC} \qquad (3)$$

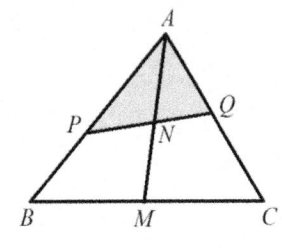

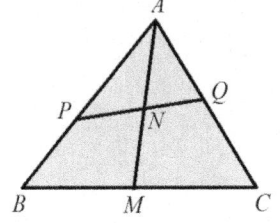

(1) + (2):

$$\frac{AP \times AN}{AB \times AM} + \frac{AQ \times AN}{AC \times AM} = \frac{S_{\triangle APN}}{S_{\triangle ABM}} + \frac{S_{\triangle AQN}}{S_{\triangle ACM}} = \frac{S_{\triangle APO}}{S_{\triangle ACM}} = \frac{2S_{\triangle APO}}{S_{\triangle ABC}} \qquad (4)$$

Substituting (3) into (4):

The Mass Points Method   Chapter 4. Splitting Mass Points

$$\frac{AP \times AN}{AB \times AM} + \frac{AQ \times AN}{AC \times AM} = \frac{S_{\triangle APQ}}{S_{\triangle ABC}} = 2 \times \frac{AP \times AQ}{AB \times AC} \qquad (5)$$

Multiply (4) by $\frac{AB \times AC \times AM}{AP \times AQ \times AN}$: $\frac{AC}{AQ} + \frac{AB}{AP} = \frac{2AM}{AN}$.

Method 3:

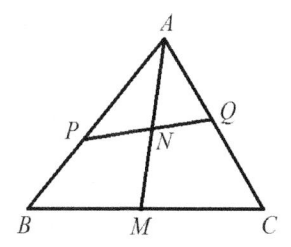

Since $BM = CM$, $S_{\triangle ABC} = 2S_{\triangle ABM} = 2S_{\triangle ACM}$

We know that $S_{\triangle APQ} = S_{\triangle APN} + S_{\triangle ANQ}$ (1)

Divide both sides of (1) by $S_{\triangle ABC}$:

$$\frac{S_{\triangle APQ}}{S_{\triangle ABC}} = \frac{S_{\triangle APN}}{S_{\triangle ABC}} + \frac{S_{\triangle ANQ}}{S_{\triangle ABC}} \qquad (2)$$

Since $BM = CM$, $S_{\triangle ABC} = 2S_{\triangle ABM} = 2S_{\triangle ACM}$ (3)

Substituting (3) into (2):

$$\frac{S_{\triangle APQ}}{S_{\triangle ABC}} = \frac{S_{\triangle APN}}{2S_{\triangle ABM}} + \frac{S_{\triangle ANQ}}{2S_{\triangle ANC}}$$

For each related triangle in (2):

$$\frac{AP \times AQ}{AB \times AC} = \frac{AP \times AN}{2AB \times AM} + \frac{AN \times AQ}{2AM \times AC} = \frac{1}{2}\left(\frac{AP}{AB} + \frac{AQ}{AC}\right)\frac{AN}{AM} \Rightarrow$$

$$\frac{2AM}{AN} = \frac{\frac{AP}{AB} + \frac{AQ}{AC}}{\frac{AP \times AQ}{AB \times AC}} = \frac{(AB \times AC)\frac{AP}{AB} + \frac{AQ}{AC}}{AP \times AQ} = \frac{(AB \times AC)\frac{AC \times AP + AB \times AQ}{AB \times AC}}{AP \times AQ}$$

$$= \frac{AC \times AP + AB \times AQ}{AP \times AQ} = \frac{AC}{AQ} + \frac{AB}{AP}.$$

The Mass Points Method   Chapter 4. Splitting Mass Points

Chapter 4. Problems

Problem 1. In triangle *ABC*, *ED* joins points *E* and *D* on the sides of *AB* and *BC*, respectively forming a transversal. *BG* divides *AC* in a ratio of 3 to 7 and intersects *ED* at point *F*. Find the ratio *BF* : *FG* if *BE* : *EA* = 3: 4 and *BD* : *DC* = 5: 2. Express your answer as a common fraction.

Problem 2. (ARML 1992 I8). In △*ABC*, points *D* and *E* are on *AB* and *AC*, respectively. The angle bisector of ∠*A* intersects *DE* at *F* and *BC* at *T* . If *AD* = 1, *DB* = 3, *AE* = 2, and *EC* = 4, compute the ratio *AF* : *AT* .

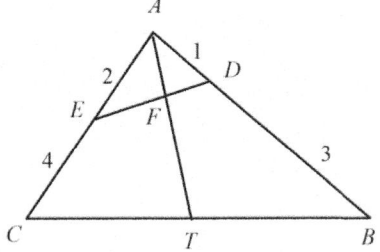

Problem 3. (Mathcounts) Triangle *ABC*, shown here, has cevian *AD* and transversal *EF* intersecting at *G*, with *AE* : *CE* = 1 : 2, *AF* : *BF* = 5 : 4 and *BD* : *CD* = 3 : 2. What is the ratio of *EG* to *FG*? Express your answer as a common fraction.

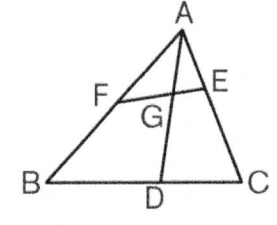

70

Problem 4. In $\triangle ABC$, D is on BC such that $BD : DC = 3 + 2$, E is on AC such that $2AE = EC$, and F and G are on AC such that $AF : FG : GB = 2 : 3 : 3$. CF and ED intersect at a point H and CG and ED intersect at a point I. Compute $\dfrac{CH}{HF} \times \dfrac{CI}{GI}$.

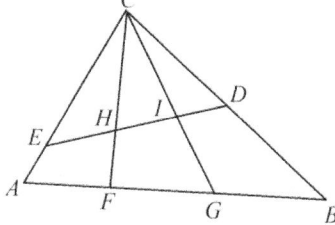

Problem 5. In triangle ABC, AD is the median on BC. EG joins points E and G on the sides of AB and AC, respectively forming a transversal to meet AD at F. Find the value of $\dfrac{EF}{EG} \times \dfrac{AD}{AF} \times \dfrac{AG}{AC}$.

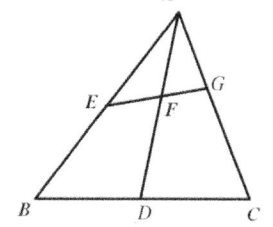

The Mass Points Method   Chapter 4. Splitting Mass Points

Chapter 4. Solutions

Problem 1. Solution: $\dfrac{75}{79}$.

(1) We label the length of each line segment as shown.
Let the masses in each point be m_A, m_B, m_C, and m_G, respectively. We need to find m_B and m_G.

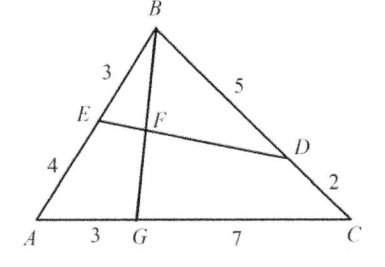

(2) We assign a mass of 105 to point A.

We look at the side BC.

$m_C \times 7 = m_A \times 3 \quad \Rightarrow \quad m_C = 45$ and

$m_G = m_B + m_C = 105 + 45 = 150$.

Now we can determine m_B by splitting masses.
We look at the side AB with E as the center of mass.

$m_{B_{AB}} \times 3 = m_A \times 4$

$\Rightarrow \quad m_{B_{AB}} = 140$

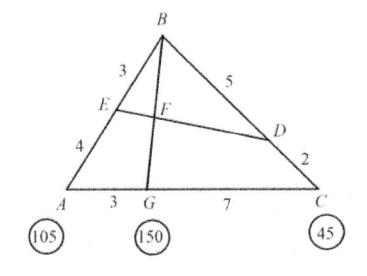

We look at the side BC with D as the center of mass.

$m_{B_{BC}} \times 5 = m_C \times 2$

$\Rightarrow \quad m_{B_{BC}} = 18$.

Thus $m_B = m_{B_{AB}} + m_{B_{BC}} = 140 + 18 = 158$

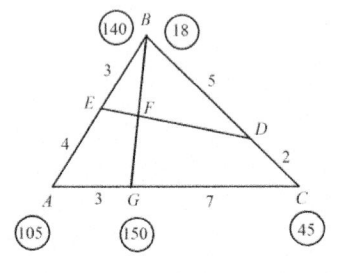

Finally, we look at the side BG with F as the center of mass, to get the answer:

$m_G \times FG = m_B \times BF \quad \Rightarrow \quad \dfrac{BF}{FG} = \dfrac{150}{158} = \dfrac{75}{79}$.

Problem 2. Solution: $\dfrac{5}{18}$.

The Mass Points Method   **Chapter 4. Splitting Mass Points**

By the Angle Bisector theorem, we have
$\frac{CT}{BT} = \frac{6}{4} = \frac{3}{2}$.

(1) We label the length of each line segment as shown.
Let the masses in each point be m_A, m_B, m_C, and m_T, respectively. We need to find m_A and m_T.

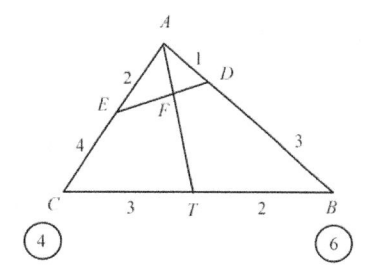

(2) We assign a mass of 4 to point C.

We look at the side BC.
$m_C \times 3 = m_B \times 2 \quad \Rightarrow \quad m_B = 6$.
$m_T = m_C + m_B = 4 + 6 = 10$.

Now we determine m_A by splitting masses.

We look at the side AC with E as the center of mass.
$m_{A_{AC}} \times 2 = m_C \times 4 \quad \Rightarrow \quad m_{A_{AC}} = 8$.

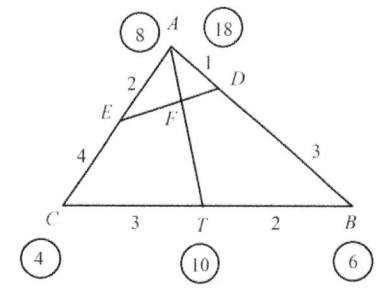

We look at the side AB with D as the center of mass.
$m_{A_{AB}} \times 1 = m_B \times 3 \quad \Rightarrow \quad m_{A_{AB}} = 18$.
Thus $m_A = m_{A_{AB}} + m_{A_{AC}} = 18 + 8 = 26$.

Finally, we look at AT with F as the center of mass to find the answer:
$m_A \times AF = m_T \times FT \quad \Rightarrow \quad \frac{FT}{AF} = \frac{26}{10} = \frac{13}{5} \quad \Rightarrow \quad \frac{AT - AF}{AF} = \frac{13}{5}$
$\Rightarrow \quad \frac{AT}{AF} - 1 = \frac{13}{5} \quad \Rightarrow \quad \frac{AT}{AF} = \frac{18}{5}$
$\Rightarrow \quad \frac{AF}{AT} = \frac{5}{18}$.

73

The Mass Points Method   Chapter 4. Splitting Mass Points

Problem 3. Solution: 2/5.
(1) We label the length of each line segment as shown. Let the masses in each point be m_A, m_B, m_C, and m_D, respectively. We need to find m_A and m_D.

(2) We assign a mass of 10 to point B.
Now we determine m_A by splitting masses.

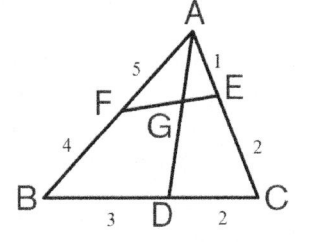

We look at the side AB, with F as the center of mass.
$m_B \times 4 = m_{A_{AB}} \times 5$
$\Rightarrow \quad m_{A_{AB}} = 8$.

We look at the side BC, with D as the center of mass.
$m_B \times 3 = m_C \times 2$
$\Rightarrow \quad m_C = 15$.
$m_D = m_B + m_C = 10 + 15 = 25$.

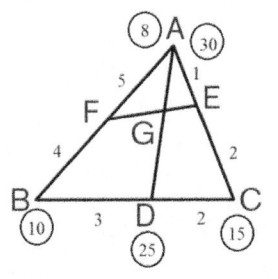

We look at the side AC, with E as the center of mass.
$m_{A_{AC}} \times 1 = m_C \times 2$
$\Rightarrow \quad m_{A_{AC}} = 30$
$m_A = m_{A_{AB}} + m_{A_{AC}} = 8 + 30 = 38$.

$m_F = m_B + m_{A_{AB}} = 10 + 8 = 18$.
$m_E = m_C + m_{A_{AC}} = 15 + 30 = 45$

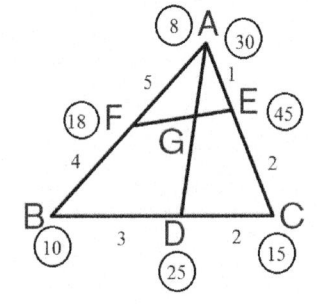

Finally, we look at the side AD, with G as the center of mass to find the answer:

$m_E \times EG = m_F \times FG$

The Mass Points Method   **Chapter 4. Splitting Mass Points**

$$\Rightarrow \quad \frac{EG}{FG} = \frac{m_F}{m_E} = \frac{18}{45} = \frac{2}{5}.$$

Problem 4. Solution: $\frac{32}{27}$.

We separate the original figure into two figures.

The first figure is obtained by removing the segment CF, as shown to the right.

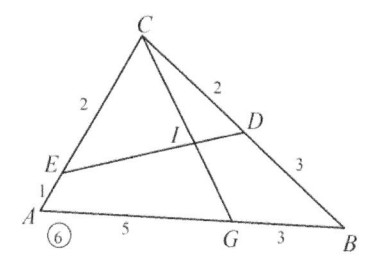

We assign a mass of 6 to point A.

$m_A \times 1 = m_{C_{AC}} \times 2$

$\Rightarrow \quad m_{C_{AC}} = 3$.

$m_A \times 5 = m_B \times 3$

$\Rightarrow \quad m_B = 5$.

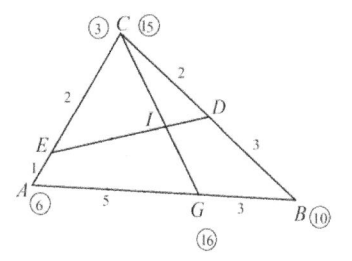

This gives us $m_{C_{BC}} = 15$.

Thus $m_G = 10 + 6 = 16$.

$m_C = 15 + 3 = 18$.

$$\frac{CI}{GI} = \frac{16}{18} = \frac{8}{9} \qquad (1)$$

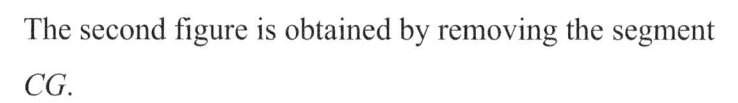

The second figure is obtained by removing the segment CG.

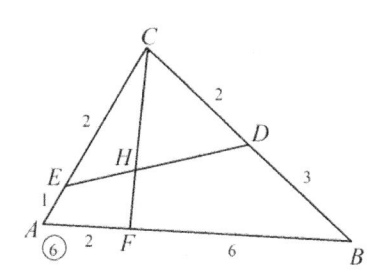

We assign a mass of 6 to point A.

$m_A \times 1 = m_{C_{AC}} \times 2$

$\Rightarrow \quad m_{C_{AC}} = 3$.

This gives us $m_E = 3 + 1 = 4$.

$m_A \times 2 = m_B \times 6$

$\Rightarrow \quad m_B = 2$.

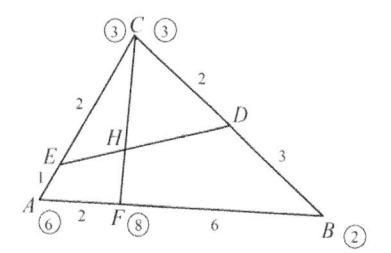

The Mass Points Method **Chapter 4. Splitting Mass Points**

It follows that $m_F = 6+2 = 8$, $m_{C_{BC}} = 3$. Thus $m_C = 3+3 = 6$.

$$\frac{CH}{HD} = \frac{8}{6} = \frac{4}{3} \quad (2)$$

$(1) \times (2)$: $\dfrac{CH}{HF} \times \dfrac{CI}{GI} = \dfrac{4}{3} \times \dfrac{8}{9} = \dfrac{32}{27}$.

Problem 5. Solution: $\dfrac{1}{2}$.

We label each line segment as shown.

We assign $m_B = 1$ and it follows that $m_C = 1$ and $m_D = 2$.

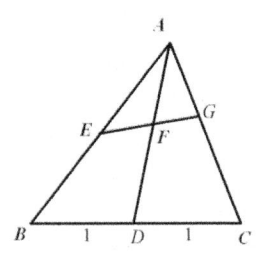

$m_E = m_{A_{AB}} + m_B = m_{A_{AB}} + 1$

$m_G = m_{A_{AC}} + m_C = m_{A_{AC}} + 1$

$m_F = m_E + m_G = m_{A_{AB}} + 1 + m_{A_{AC}} + 1 = m_A + 2$.

$$\frac{EF}{EG} = \frac{m_G}{m_F} = \frac{m_{A_{AC}} + 1}{m_A + 2} \quad (1)$$

$$\frac{AD}{AF} = \frac{m_F}{m_D} = \frac{m_A + 2}{2} \quad (2)$$

$$\frac{AG}{AC} = \frac{m_C}{m_G} = \frac{1}{m_{A_{AC}} + 1} \quad (3)$$

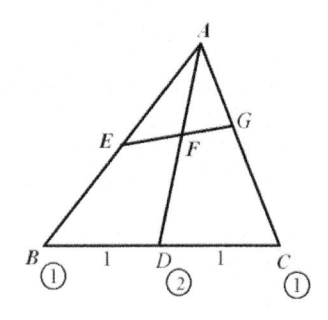

$(1) \times (2)$: $\dfrac{EF}{EG} \times \dfrac{AD}{AF} = \dfrac{m_{A_{AC}} + 1}{m_A + 2} \times \dfrac{m_A + 2}{2} = \dfrac{m_{A_{AC}} + 1}{2} \quad (4)$

$(3) \times (4)$: $\dfrac{EF}{EG} \times \dfrac{AD}{AF} \times \dfrac{AG}{AC} = \dfrac{1}{2}$.

The Mass Points Method **Chapter 5. Length and Area Problems**

Chapter 5. Length and Area Problems

Example 1. (2019 AMC 8 Problem 24) In triangle ABC, point D divides side AC so that $\dfrac{AD}{DC} = \dfrac{1}{2}$. Let E be the midpoint of BD and let F be the point of intersection of line BC and line AE. Given that the area of triangle ABC is 360, what is the area of triangle EBF?

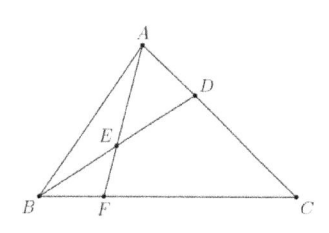

Solution: 30.

Since $\dfrac{AD}{DC} = \dfrac{1}{2}$, $\dfrac{S_{\triangle ABD}}{S_{\triangle ABC}} = \dfrac{1}{3}$, $S_{\triangle ABD} = \dfrac{1}{3} S_{\triangle ABC} = 120$,

$S_{\triangle ABE} = \dfrac{1}{2} S_{\triangle ABD} = 60$.

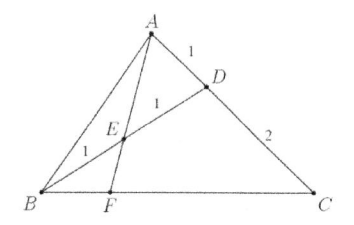

We assign 1 as the mass to point C.
Then we get $m_A = 2$, $m_D = 3$, $m_B = 3$, $m_F = 4$.

$\dfrac{S_{\triangle BEF}}{S_{\triangle ABE}} = \dfrac{EF}{EA} = \dfrac{m_A}{m_F} = \dfrac{2}{4} = \dfrac{1}{2}$

$\Rightarrow \quad S_{\triangle BEF} = \dfrac{1}{2} S_{\triangle ABE} = 30$.

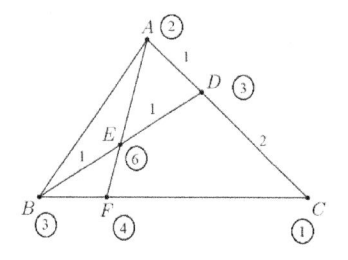

Example 2. In triangle ABC, point D divides side AC so that $\dfrac{AD}{DC} = \dfrac{1}{2}$. Let E be the midpoint of BD and let F be the point of intersection of line BC and line AE. Given that the area of triangle ABC is 360, what is the area of quadrilateral $CDEF$?

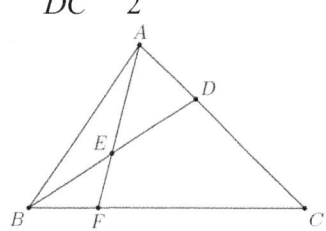

Solution: 30.

Since $\dfrac{AD}{DC} = \dfrac{1}{2}$, $\dfrac{S_{\triangle ABD}}{S_{\triangle ABC}} = \dfrac{1}{3}$, $S_{\triangle ABD} = \dfrac{1}{3} S_{\triangle ABC} = 120$,

The Mass Points Method   **Chapter 5. Length and Area Problems**

$S_{\triangle ABE} = \dfrac{1}{2} S_{\triangle ABD} = 60$.

We assign 1 as the mass to point C.

Then we get $m_A = 2$, $m_D = 3$, $m_B = 3$, $m_F = 4$.

$\dfrac{S_{\triangle BEF}}{S_{\triangle ABE}} = \dfrac{EF}{EA} = \dfrac{m_A}{m_F} = \dfrac{2}{4} = \dfrac{1}{2} \Rightarrow S_{\triangle BEF} = \dfrac{1}{2} S_{\triangle ABE} = 30$.

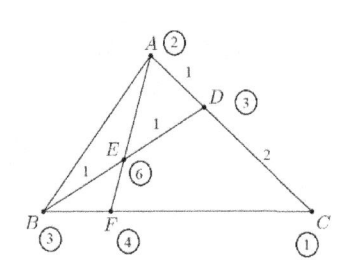

Example 3. (AMC) In triangle ABC, BD is a median. CF intersects BD at E so that the length of BE is equal to the length of ED. Point F is on AB. Then, if $\overline{BF} = 5$, $\overline{BA}$ equals:
(A) 10   (B) 12   (C) 15   (D) 20   (E) none of these

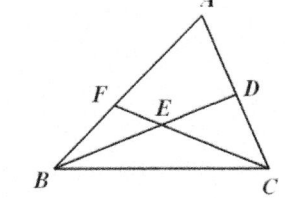

Solution: C.
We use a different method from the official solution to solve this problem.

We label the length of each line segment as shown.

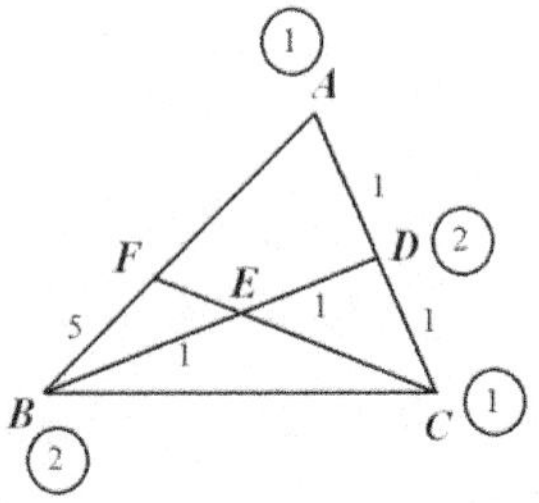

We assign a mass of 1 to point C.

$m_A \times 1 = m_C \times 1 \qquad \Rightarrow \qquad m_A = 1$ and

$m_D = m_A + m_C = 1 + 1 = 2$.

Since $BE = DE$, $m_B \times 1 = m_D \times 1 \Rightarrow m_B = 2$.

Now we look at the line segment AB:

$m_A \times AF = m_B \times 5 \qquad \Rightarrow \qquad AF = \dfrac{2 \times 5}{1} = 10$

It follows that $AB = BF + AF = 5 + 10 = 15$.

78

The Mass Points Method **Chapter 5. Length and Area Problems**

Example 4. As shown in the figure, $\triangle ABC$ is divided into three smaller triangles (with the areas of 5, 8, and 10 as indicated in the figure) and one quadrilateral of the area x. Find x.

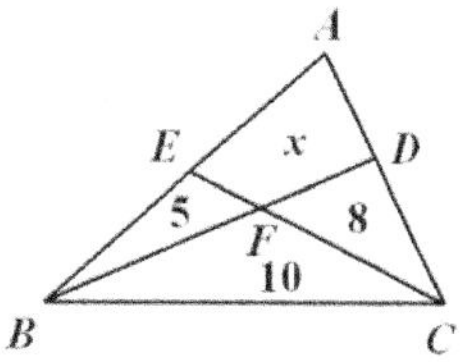

Solution: 22.
Method 1:
$$\frac{S_{\triangle BCF}}{S_{\triangle DCF}} = \frac{BF}{DF} = \frac{10}{8} = \frac{5}{4}, \quad \frac{S_{\triangle BEF}}{S_{\triangle BCF}} = \frac{EF}{CF} = \frac{5}{10} = \frac{1}{2}.$$

We label the length of each line segment as shown.

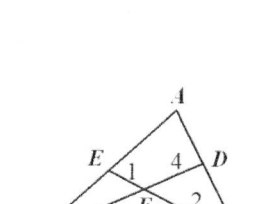

We assign a mass of 4 to point B.
$m_B \times BF = m_D \times DF \Rightarrow m_D = 5$ and
$m_F = m_D + m_B = 5 + 4 = 9$.

Now we look at the line segment EC:
$m_E \times 1 = m_C \times 2$ (1)
$m_E + m_C = 9$ (2)
Solving (1) and (2): $m_e = 6$.
Since $m_E = m_A + m_B$, $m_A = 2$.

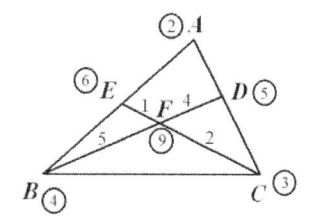

Now we look at the line segment AB:
$m_B \times BE = m_A \times AE \Rightarrow \frac{AE}{BE} = \frac{4}{2} = 2$.
$\frac{S_{\triangle CAE}}{S_{\triangle CBE}} = \frac{AE}{BE} = \frac{4}{2} = 2 \Rightarrow S_{\triangle CAE} = 2 S_{\triangle CBE}$
$\Rightarrow \quad x + 8 = 2(5 + 10) \Rightarrow x = 30 - 8 = 22$.

Method 2:
$\frac{S_{\triangle ABC}}{S_{\triangle CBD}} = \frac{AC}{CD} = \frac{m_D}{m_A}$.

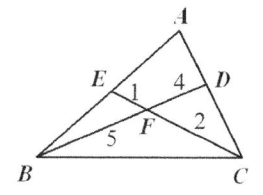

The Mass Points Method   **Chapter 5. Length and Area Problems**

$$\frac{S_{\Delta BCF}}{S_{\Delta DCF}} = \frac{BF}{DF} = \frac{10}{8} = \frac{5}{4} \cdot \frac{S_{\Delta BEF}}{S_{\Delta BCF}} = \frac{EF}{CF} = \frac{5}{10} = \frac{1}{2}.$$

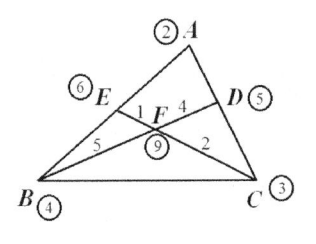

We label the length of each line segment as shown. We assign a mass of 4 to point B. It follows that $m_D = 5$, $m_F = 9$, $m_E = 6$, and $m_A = 2$.

$$\frac{S_{\Delta ABC}}{S_{\Delta CBD}} = \frac{m_D}{m_A} = \frac{5}{2} \Rightarrow S_{\Delta ABC} = \frac{5}{2} S_{\Delta CBD} = \frac{5}{2} \times 18 = 45.$$

$x = 45 - 10 - 8 - 5 = 22$.

Example 5. (2006 AMC 10 B Problem 23) A triangle is partitioned into three triangles and a quadrilateral by drawing two lines from vertices to their opposite sides. The areas of the three triangles are 3, 7, and 7, as shown. What is the area of the shaded quadrilateral?
(A) 15 (B) 17 (C) 35/2 (D) 18 (E) 55/3

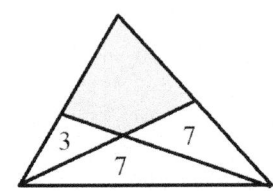

Solution: (D).
Method 1:
First we label the line segments as follows and then we assign the mass of $m_c = 1$.

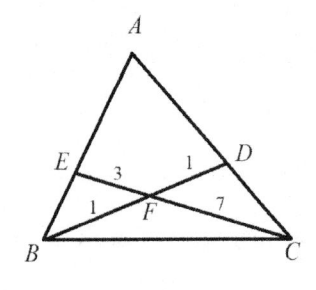

It follows that $m_E = 7$, $m_F = 10$, $m_B = 5$, $m_D = 5$, $m_A = 2$.

$$\frac{S_{\Delta ACE}}{S_{\Delta BCE}} = \frac{AE}{BE} = \frac{m_B}{m_A} = \frac{5}{2} \Rightarrow$$

$$S_{\Delta ACE} = \frac{5}{2} S_{\Delta BCE} = \frac{5}{2} \times (3+7) = 25.$$

The answer is $S_{\Delta ACE} - S_{\Delta ACDF} = 25 - 7 = 18$.

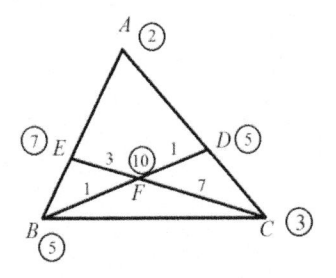

Method 2:

The Mass Points Method   Chapter 5. Length and Area Problems

$$\frac{S_{\triangle ABD}}{S_{\triangle CBD}} = \frac{AD}{DC} = \frac{m_C}{m_A}.$$

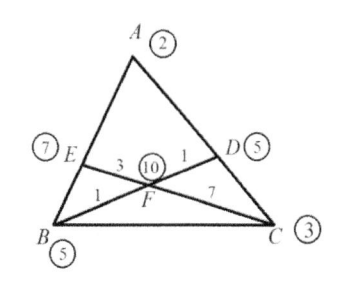

First we label the line segments.

Then we assign the mass:

We assign $m_c = 3$.

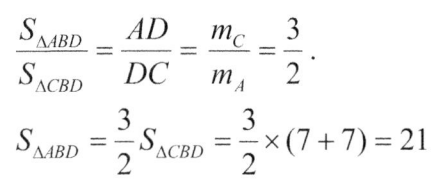

We calculate $m_E = 7$, $m_F = 10$, $m_B = 5$, $m_A = 2$.

$$\frac{S_{\triangle ABD}}{S_{\triangle CBD}} = \frac{AD}{DC} = \frac{m_C}{m_A} = \frac{3}{2}.$$

$$S_{\triangle ABD} = \frac{3}{2} S_{\triangle CBD} = \frac{3}{2} \times (7+7) = 21$$

The answer is $S_{\triangle ABD} - S_{\triangle BEF} = 21 - 3 = 18$.

Example 6. As shown in the figure, $\triangle ABC$ is divided into three smaller triangles and one quadrilateral of the area x. $3AE = 2EB$. $3AD = 2DC$. Find x if the area of $\triangle ABC$ is 70.

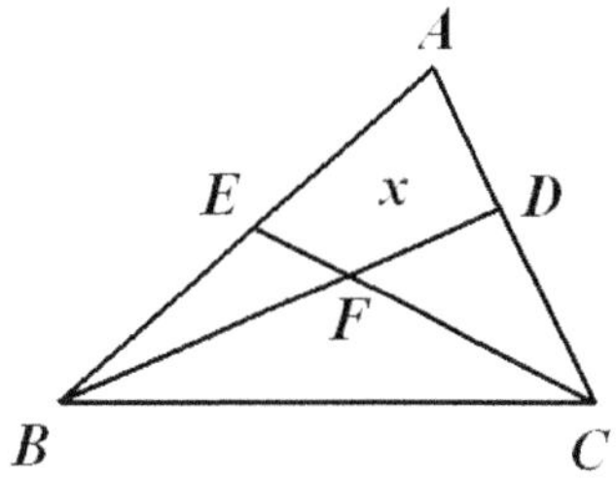

Solution: 16.
We label the length of each line segment as shown.
We assign a mass of 3 to point A.

$m_A \times 2 = m_C \times 3$

$\Rightarrow \quad m_C = 2$ and $m_D = m_A + m_C = 3 + 2 = 5$.

Since $3AE = 2BE$, $m_B = 2$.

Now we look at the line segment BD:
$m_B \times BF = m_D \times FD$

$\Rightarrow \quad \dfrac{FD}{BF} = \dfrac{2}{5} \quad \Rightarrow \dfrac{FD}{BD} = \dfrac{2}{7}.$

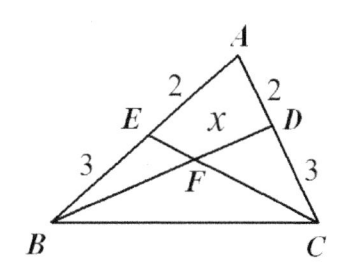

The Mass Points Method Chapter 5. Length and Area Problems

$$\frac{S_{\triangle CDF}}{S_{\triangle CDB}} = \frac{FD}{BD} = \frac{2}{7}$$

$$\Rightarrow S_{\triangle CDF} = \frac{2}{7} S_{\triangle CDB} = \frac{2}{7} \times \frac{3}{5} S_{\triangle ABC} = 12.$$

$$S_{\triangle ACE} = \frac{2}{5} S_{\triangle ABC} = \frac{2}{5} \times 70 = 28$$

$$x = S_{\triangle ACE} - S_{\triangle Cdf} = 28 - 12 = 16.$$

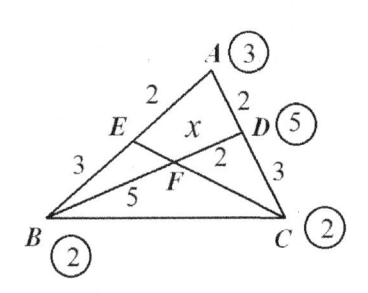

Example 7. In triangle *ABC*, with $\angle A = 70°$, a point *D* is taken on *AC*. The angle bisector of $\angle A$ meets *BD* at *H* ad meets *BC* at *E*. $AF : FE = 3 : 1$, $BF : FD = 5 : 3$. Find the value of $\angle C$.
(A) 70° (B) 45° (C) 55° (D) 75° (E) 80°

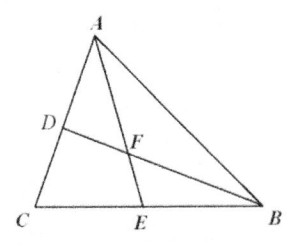

Solution:
We label each line segment as shown.
We assign $m_B = 3$. It follows that $m_D = 5$, $m_F = 8$, and $m_A = 2$ and $m_E = 6$.

$$\frac{CE}{EB} = \frac{m_B}{m_C} = \frac{3}{3} = 1, \text{ so } CE = EB.$$

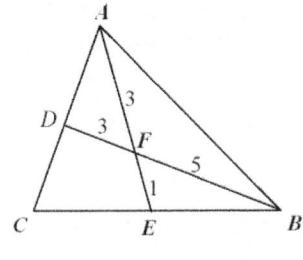

This means that *AE* is both the angle bisector and the median. Thus *AE* is the perpendicular bisector of *BC*. Therefore, triangle *ABC* is an isosceles triangle with

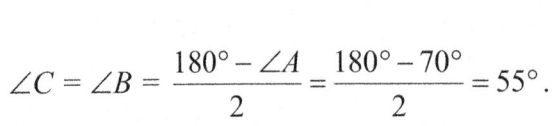

$$\angle C = \angle B = \frac{180° - \angle A}{2} = \frac{180° - 70°}{2} = 55°.$$

The answer is (C).

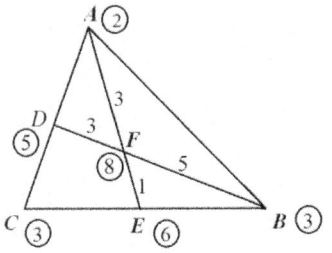

The Mass Points Method   **Chapter 5. Length and Area Problems**

Example 8. As shown in the figure, $\triangle ABC$ is divided into three smaller triangles and one quadrilateral. If $\dfrac{BD}{DC} = \dfrac{m}{1}$, $\dfrac{CE}{EA} = \dfrac{n}{1}$, find $\dfrac{S_{\triangle ABF}}{S_{\triangle ABC}}$ in terms of m and n. Express your answer as a common fraction.

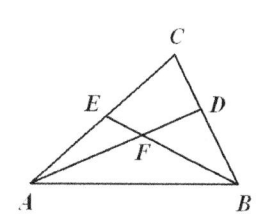

Solution: $\dfrac{m}{mn+1+m}$.

We label the length of each line segment as shown.

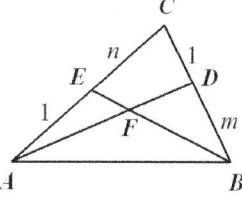

Next, we connect CF and extend it to meet AB at G.

We assign a mass of 1 to point B.

$m_B \times m = m_C \times 1 \Rightarrow m_C = m$.

Now we look at the line segment AC.
$m_C \times n = m_A \times 1$
$\Rightarrow \quad m_A = mn \quad (1)$

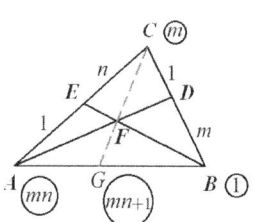

Now we look at the line segment AB. Since F is the center mass of ABC, G is the center of mass of A and B, so $m_G = m_A + m_B = mn+1$.

$\dfrac{S_{\triangle ABF}}{S_{\triangle ABC}} = \dfrac{FG}{CG} = \dfrac{m}{mn+1+m}$.

Example 9. (AIME) As shown in the figure on the right, $\triangle ABC$ is divided into six smaller triangles by lines drawn from the vertices through a common interior point. The areas of four of these triangles are as indicated. Find the area of $\triangle ABC$.

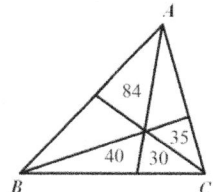

83

The Mass Points Method Chapter 5. Length and Area Problems

Solution: 315.
We use a different method from the official solution to solve this problem.

$$\frac{S_{\triangle BPD}}{S_{\triangle CPD}} = \frac{40}{30} = \frac{BD}{DC} = \frac{4}{3}.$$

$$\frac{S_{\triangle BPC}}{S_{\triangle EPC}} = \frac{40+30}{35} = \frac{BP}{PE} = \frac{2}{1}.$$

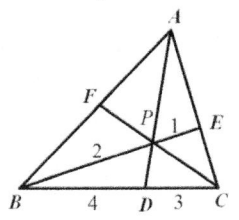

We label the length of each line segment as shown.
Let the masses in each point be m_A, m_B, m_C, and m_E, respectively.

We assign a mass of 4 to point C.
We look at the line segment BE.
$m_B \times 2 = m_E \times 1 \Rightarrow \quad m_E = 6$.

Now we look at the line segment AC.
$m_A = m_E - m_C = 6 - 4 = 2$

$\frac{AE}{CE} = \frac{4}{2} = 2$. So $\frac{AC}{CE} = 3$.

$\frac{S_{\triangle ABC}}{S_{\triangle EBC}} = \frac{AC}{CE} = 3$

$\Rightarrow \quad S_{\triangle ABC} = 3 S_{\triangle EBC} = 3(40+30+35) = 315$.

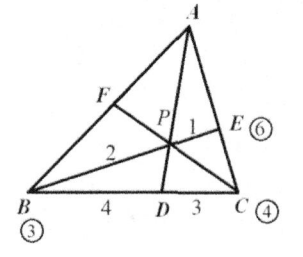

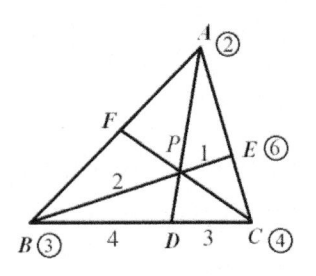

Example 10. (ARML 1989 T4). In $\triangle ABC$, angle bisectors AD and BE intersect at P. If the sides of the triangle are $a = 3$, $b = 5$, $c = 7$, with $BP = x$, and $PE = y$, compute the ratio $x : y$, where x and y are relatively prime integers.

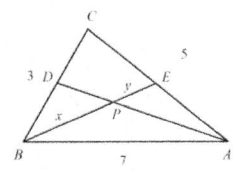

84

The Mass Points Method Chapter 5. Length and Area Problems

Solution: 2.

$$\frac{x}{y} = \frac{BP}{PE} = \frac{m_E}{m_B}$$

Since we want to find $BP : PE$, we need to find the masses of B and E.

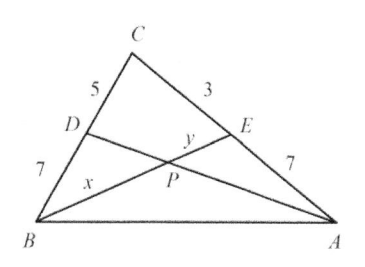

By the Angle Bisector theorem, we have
$\frac{CE}{AE} = \frac{3}{7}$, and $\frac{BD}{CD} = \frac{7}{5}$.

Then we label the length of each line segment as shown.

Let the masses in each point be m_A, m_B, m_C, and m_E, respectively.

We want to find m_B and m_E.

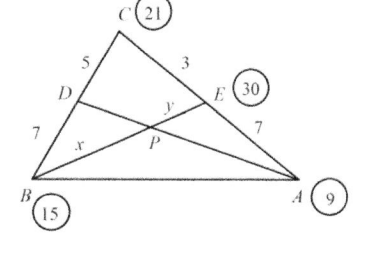

We assign a mass of 15 to point B.

We look at the side BC.

$m_B \times 7 = m_C \times 5 \quad \Rightarrow \quad m_C = 21$.

Next, we determine m_A by looking at the side AC. The center of mass of AC is on E.

$m_C \times 3 = m_A \times 7 \quad \Rightarrow \quad m_A = 9$

$m_E = m_A + m_C = 9 + 21 = 30$.

Finally, we look at side BE to get the answer:

$$\frac{x}{y} = \frac{BP}{PE} = \frac{m_E}{m_B} = \frac{30}{15} = 2.$$

Example 11. (AMC) The sides of a triangle are of lengths 13, 14, and 15. The altitudes of the triangle meet at point H. If AD is the altitude to side of length 14, the ratio $HD : HA$ is:
(A) 3: 11 (B) 5: 11 (C) 1:2 (D) 2:3 (E) 25:33

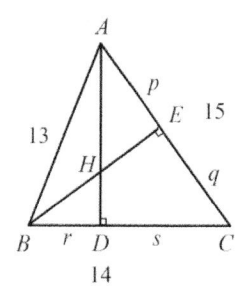

The Mass Points Method **Chapter 5. Length and Area Problems**

Solution: B.

$$\frac{HD}{HA} = \frac{m_A}{m_D}$$

We use a different method from the official solution to solve this problem.

Applying Pythagorean Theorem to triangles *ABE* and *BCE*, we have
$BE^2 = 14^2 - q^2 = 13^2 - p^2 \Rightarrow q^2 - p^2 = 27$.
We know that $q + p = 15$.
So $p = \frac{33}{5}$, $q = \frac{42}{5}$, giving us $\frac{p}{q} = \frac{11}{14}$.

Applying Pythagorean Theorem to triangles *ABD* and *ACD*, we have

$AD^2 = 13^2 - r^2 = 15^2 - s^2 \Rightarrow s^2 - r^2 = (s+r)(s-r) = 56$.
Since we are given $s + r = 14$, $s - r = 4$, and it follows that $r = 5$ and $s = 9$, and so $\frac{r}{s} = \frac{5}{9}$.

Now we are ready to use the mass points method.
We label the known length of each line segment as shown.

Let the masses in each point be m_A, m_B, m_C, and m_D, respectively. In order to find *HD* : *HA*, we need to find m_B and m_E.

We assign a mass of 55 to point *C*.

We look at the side *AC*. The center of mass of *AC* is on *E*.
$m_C \times 14 = m_A \times 11 \quad \Rightarrow \quad m_A = 70$.

Now we determine m_B.

We look at the side *BC*. The center of mass of *BC* is on *D*.
$m_C \times 9 = m_B \times 5$
$\Rightarrow \quad m_B = 99$.

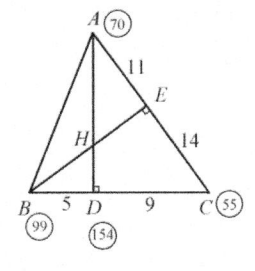

86

The Mass Points Method   **Chapter 5. Length and Area Problems**

$m_D = m_B + m_C = 99 + 55 = 154$.

Finally, we look at side *AD* to determine the answer:

$m_A \times HA = m_D \times HD \Rightarrow \dfrac{HD}{HA} = \dfrac{m_A}{m_D} = \dfrac{70}{154} = \dfrac{5}{11}$.

Example 12. (Mathcounts) In triangle *ABC*, *AD* : *BD* = 1 : 2, *BE* : *EC* = 1 : 3 and *AF* : *CF* = 3 : 2. What is the ratio of the area of triangle *GHI* to the area of triangle *ABC*? Express your answer as a common fraction.

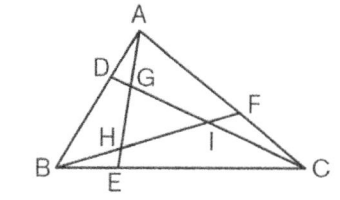

Solution: 16/105.

Let the area of triangle *ABC* be 60.

To find the area of triangle *GHI*, we determine the areas of △*BCI*, △*ACG*, and △*ABH*, and then subtract their sum from the area of △*ABC*.

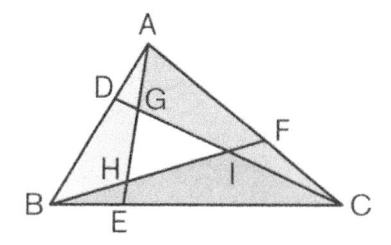

We separate the original figure into three figures.

The first figure is obtained by removing the segment *AE*.

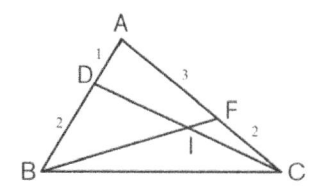

We label the length of each line segment as shown. We assign a mass of 1 to point *B*.

$m_B \times 2 = m_A \times 1 \quad \Rightarrow \quad m_A = 2$.

Now we look at the line segment *AC*:

$m_A \times AF = m_C \times CF$

$\Rightarrow 2 \times 3 = m_C \times 2$

$\Rightarrow m_C = 3$.

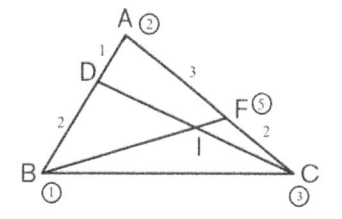

87

The Mass Points Method   **Chapter 5. Length and Area Problems**

$m_F = m_A + m_C = 2 + 3 = 5$.

Next, we look at the line segment *BF*:

$m_B \times BI = m_F \times IF \quad \Rightarrow \quad \dfrac{BI}{IF} = \dfrac{m_F}{m_B} = \dfrac{5}{1}$.

$\dfrac{S_{\Delta BCF}}{S_{\Delta ABC}} = \dfrac{CF}{CA} = \dfrac{2}{5} \quad \Rightarrow S_{\Delta BCF} = \dfrac{2}{5} S_{\Delta ABC} = 24$.

$\dfrac{S_{\Delta BCI}}{S_{\Delta BCF}} = \dfrac{BI}{BF} = \dfrac{5}{6} \quad \Rightarrow S_{\Delta BCI} = \dfrac{5}{6} S_{\Delta BCF} = \dfrac{1}{3} S_{\Delta ABC} = 20$.

The second figure is obtained by removing the segment *BF*.

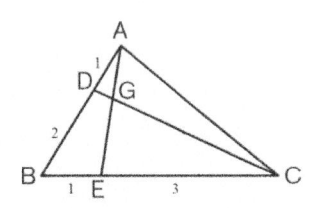

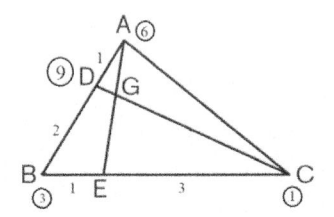

The third figure is obtained by removing the segment *CD*.

From these figures, we get $S_{\Delta ACG} = \dfrac{3}{10} S_{\Delta ABC} = 18$, and

$S_{\Delta ABH} = \dfrac{3}{14} S_{\Delta ABC} = \dfrac{90}{7}$.

$S_{\Delta GHI} = 60 - 20 - 18 - \dfrac{90}{7} = \dfrac{64}{7}$.

$\dfrac{S_{\Delta GHI}}{S_{\Delta ABC}} = \dfrac{\frac{64}{7}}{60} = \dfrac{16}{105}$.

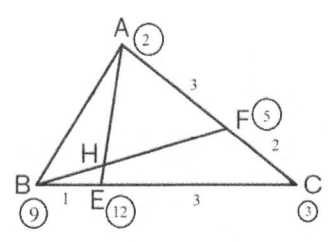

Example 13. As shown in the figure, *D* and *E* are points on *BC* of triangle *ABC* such that *BD* : *DE* : *EC* = 3:2:1. The line segment *BM* meets *AD* and *AE* at *H* and *G*

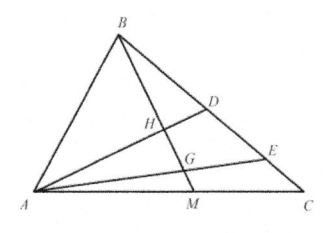

88

The Mass Points Method   **Chapter 5. Length and Area Problems**

respectively and divides AC into the ratio of $2:1$. Find $\dfrac{S_{\triangle AGH}}{S_{\triangle ABC}}$.

Solution: $\dfrac{16}{85}$.

Method 1:

We calculate $S_{\triangle ABH}$ and $S_{\triangle AGM}$ to obtain the value of $S_{\triangle AGH} = S_{\triangle AGM} - S_{\triangle ABH} - S_{\triangle AGM}$ and find the ratio.

Let the area of triangle ABC be 60.

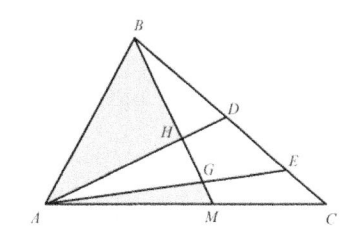

Since M divides AC into the ratio of $2:1$, the area of triangle ABM is then 40.

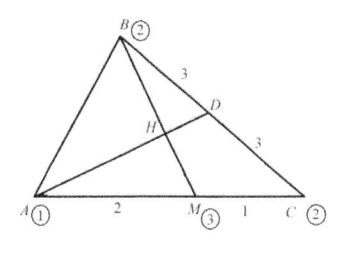

We remove the segment AE.

We assign a mass of 1 to point A.

$m_A \times 2 = m_C \times 1$

$\Rightarrow \quad m_C = 2$.

It follows that $m_B = 2$.

Thus $m_M = 1 + 2 = 3$.

$\dfrac{S_{\triangle ABH}}{S_{\triangle ACM}} = \dfrac{BH}{BC} = \dfrac{m_M}{m_H} = \dfrac{3}{5} \qquad \Rightarrow S_{\triangle ABH} = \dfrac{3}{5} S_{\triangle ACM} = 24$.

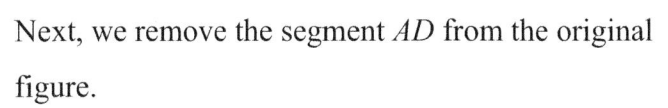

Next, we remove the segment AD from the original figure.

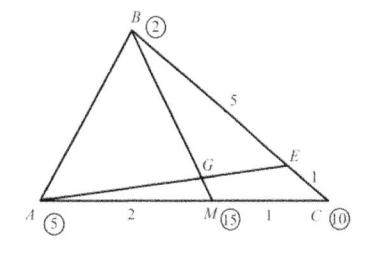

We assign a mass of 10 to point C.

$m_A \times 2 = m_C \times 1$

$\Rightarrow \quad m_A = 5$.

It follows that $m_B = 2$.

Thus $m_M = 10 + 5 = 15$ and $m_G = 17$.

The Mass Points Method **Chapter 5. Length and Area Problems**

$$\frac{S_{\triangle AGM}}{S_{\triangle ACM}} = \frac{GM}{MB} = \frac{m_B}{m_G} = \frac{2}{17} \Rightarrow S_{\triangle AGM} = \frac{2}{17} S_{\triangle ACM} = \frac{80}{17}.$$

$$S_{\triangle AGH} = S_{\triangle AGM} - S_{\triangle ABH} - S_{\triangle AGM} = 40 - 24 - \frac{80}{17} = \frac{192}{17}$$

$$\frac{S_{\triangle AGH}}{S_{\triangle ABC}} = \frac{\frac{192}{17}}{60} = \frac{16}{85}.$$

Method 2:

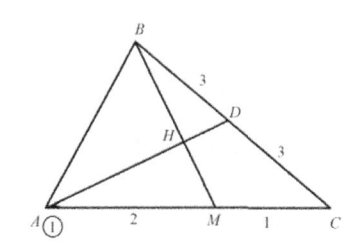

We separate the original figure into two figures.

The first figure is obtained by removing the segment AE.

We assign a mass of 1 to point A.

$m_A \times 2 = m_C \times 1$

$\Rightarrow \quad m_C = 2.$

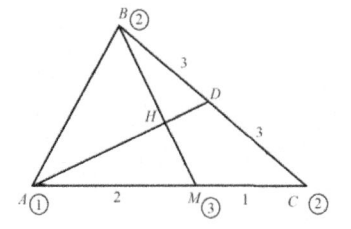

It follows that $m_B = 2$.

Thus $m_M = 1 + 2 = 3$.

$\dfrac{BH}{HM} = \dfrac{3}{2}$ and $\dfrac{BH}{BM} = \dfrac{3}{5} = \dfrac{51}{85}$

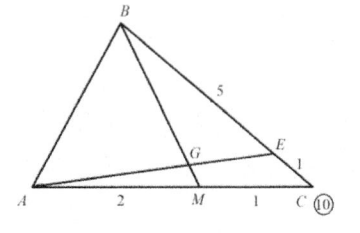

The second figure is obtained by removing the segment AD from the original figure.

We assign a mass of 10 to point C.

$m_A \times 2 = m_C \times 1$

$\Rightarrow \quad m_A = 5.$

It follows that $m_B = 2$.

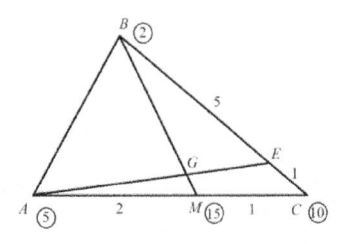

Thus $m_M = 10 + 5 = 15$.

$\dfrac{BG}{GM} = \dfrac{15}{2}$ and $\dfrac{BG}{BM} = \dfrac{15}{17} = \dfrac{75}{85}$

Thus $\dfrac{HG}{BM} = \dfrac{BG - BH}{BM} = \dfrac{24}{85}$

Now we can apply what we have found to solve the problem.

Let the area of triangle ABC be 60.

Since M divides AC into the ratio of $2 : 1$, the area of triangle ABM is then 40.

Since $\dfrac{HG}{BM} = \dfrac{24}{85}$, $\dfrac{S_{\triangle AGH}}{S_{\triangle ABM}} = \dfrac{24}{85}$

$\Rightarrow S_{\triangle AGH} = \dfrac{24}{85} \times 40 = \dfrac{192}{17}$.

$\dfrac{S_{\triangle AGH}}{S_{\triangle ABC}} = \dfrac{\frac{192}{17}}{60} = \dfrac{16}{85}$.

Example 14. In $\triangle ABC$, D is on BC such that $BD = DC$, E is on AC such that $3AE = EC$, and F and G are on AC such that $AF : FG : GB = 2 : 3 : 3$. CF and ED intersect at a point H and CG and ED intersect at a point I. Compute $EH : HI : ID$.

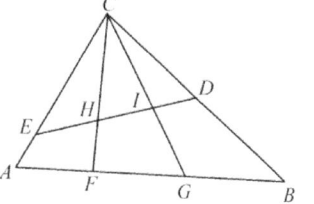

Solution: $7 : 8 : 6$.

We separate the original figure into two figures.

The first figure is obtained by removing the segment CF.

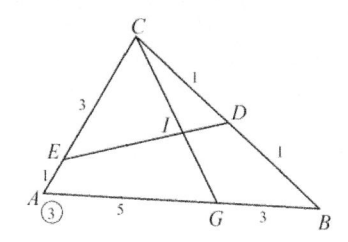

The Mass Points Method   **Chapter 5. Length and Area Problems**

We assign a mass of 3 to point A.

$m_A \times 1 = m_{C_{AC}} \times 3$

$\Rightarrow \quad m_{C_{AC}} = 1$.

It follows that $m_E = 3 + 1 = 4$.

$m_A \times 5 = m_B \times 3$

$\Rightarrow \quad m_B = 5$.

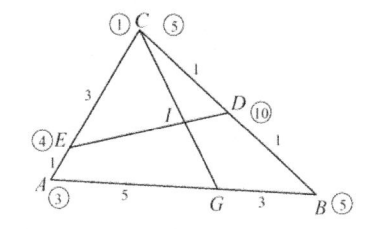

We get $m_{C_{BC}} = 5$. Thus $m_D = 5 + 5 = 10$.

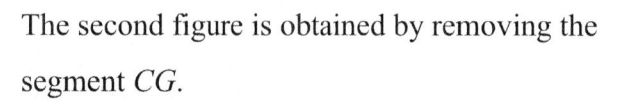

$\dfrac{EI}{ED} = \dfrac{10}{14} = \dfrac{5}{7} = \dfrac{15}{21}$.

The second figure is obtained by removing the segment CG.

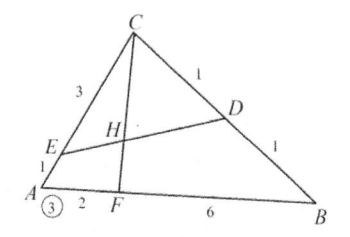

We assign a mass of 3 to point A.

$m_A \times 1 = m_{C_{AC}} \times 3$

$\Rightarrow \quad m_{C_{AC}} = 1$.

We get $m_E = 3 + 1 = 4$.

$m_A \times 2 = m_B \times 6$

$\Rightarrow \quad m_B = 1$.

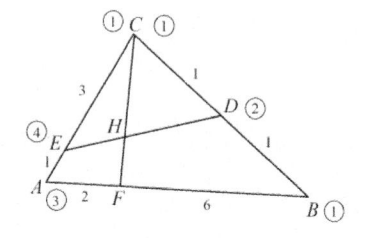

It follows that $m_{C_{BC}} = 2$. Thus $m_D = 1 + 1 = 2$.

$\dfrac{EH}{ED} = \dfrac{2}{6} = \dfrac{1}{3} = \dfrac{7}{21}$.

If $ED = 21$, $EH = 7$, $EI = 15$, then $HI = 15 - 7 = 8$, and $ID = 21 - 7 - 8 = 6$.

The answer is $7 : 8 : 6$.

Example 15. In $\triangle ABC$, points M and N trisect the sides AB, and points X and Y trisect the sides BC. AY meets BM and BN at S and R, respectively. Find the ratio of the area of quadrilateral $MNRS$ to the area of triangle ABC.

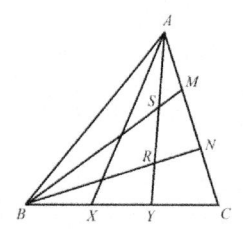

The Mass Points Method Chapter 5. Length and Area Problems

Solution: $\dfrac{5}{42}$.

$S_{\triangle ABM} = \dfrac{1}{3} S_{\triangle ABC}$

We remove the line segments AX and BN and label the line segments.
Next, we assign the mass.

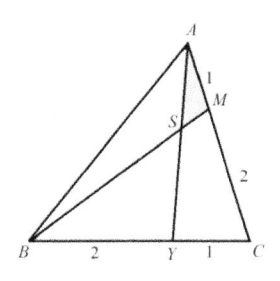

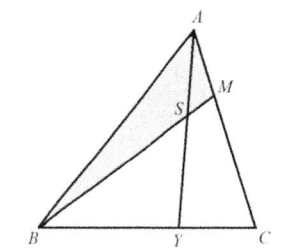

Let's assign $m_B = 1$.
It follows that $m_C = 2$, $m_A = 4$, $m_M = 6$.
$m_S = 7$.

$\dfrac{S_{\triangle AMS}}{S_{\triangle AMB}} = \dfrac{MS}{MB} = \dfrac{m_B}{m_S} = \dfrac{1}{7}$

$\Rightarrow S_{\triangle AMS} = \dfrac{1}{7} S_{\triangle AMM} = \dfrac{1}{7} \times \dfrac{1}{3} S_{\triangle ABC} = \dfrac{1}{21} S_{\triangle ABC}$ (1)

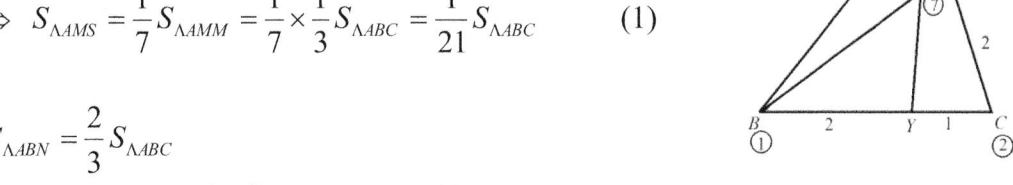

$S_{\triangle ABN} = \dfrac{2}{3} S_{\triangle ABC}$

Next, we remove the line segments AX and BM and label the line segments. Then we assign the mass.

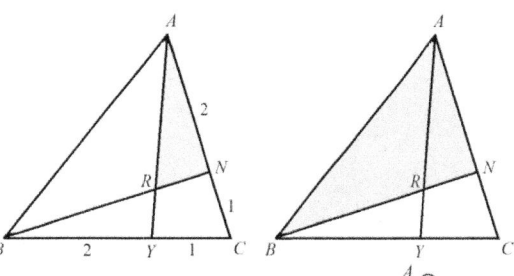

Let's assign $m_B = 1$.
It follows that $m_C = 2$, $m_A = 1$, $m_N = 5$.
$m_R = 4$.

$\dfrac{S_{\triangle ANR}}{S_{\triangle ABN}} = \dfrac{RN}{BN} = \dfrac{m_B}{m_R} = \dfrac{1}{4}$

$\Rightarrow S_{\triangle ANR} = \dfrac{1}{4} S_{\triangle ABN} = \dfrac{1}{4} \times \dfrac{2}{3} S_{\triangle ABC} = \dfrac{1}{6} S_{\triangle ABC}$ (1)

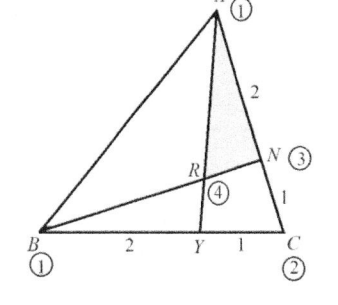

$S_{MNRS} = S_{\triangle ANR} - S_{\triangle AMS} = \dfrac{1}{6} S_{\triangle ABC} - \dfrac{1}{21} S_{\triangle ABC} = \dfrac{5}{42} S_{\triangle ABC}$.

The Mass Points Method   **Chapter 5. Length and Area Problems**

Therefore, $\dfrac{S_{MNRS}}{S_{\triangle ABC}} = \dfrac{5}{42}$.

Example 16. Isosceles right triangle ABC has $\angle C = 90°$. M is a point on CB such that $CM = 2MB$. $CP \perp AB$. Find the value of $\dfrac{AP}{PB}$.

Solution: $\dfrac{3}{2}$.

$\dfrac{AP}{PB} = \dfrac{m_B}{m_A}$.

We know that $\dfrac{CM}{MB} = \dfrac{2}{1}$

$AM = \sqrt{2^2 + 3^2} = \sqrt{13}$

$CM^2 = AM \times MN \quad \Rightarrow \quad 2^2 = \sqrt{13} \times MN \quad \Rightarrow$

$MN = \dfrac{4}{\sqrt{13}}$.

$AC^2 = AM \times AN \quad \Rightarrow \quad 3^2 = \sqrt{13} \times AN \quad \Rightarrow$

$AN = \dfrac{9}{\sqrt{13}}$.

$\dfrac{AN}{MN} = \dfrac{\frac{9}{\sqrt{13}}}{\frac{4}{\sqrt{13}}} = \dfrac{9}{4}$.

We label each line segment as shown.

We assign $m_B = 12$. We get $m_C = 6$, $m_M = 18$, $m_A = 8$. Then $m_P = 20$.

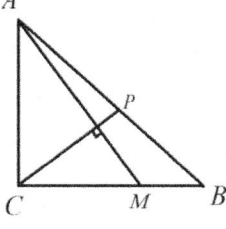

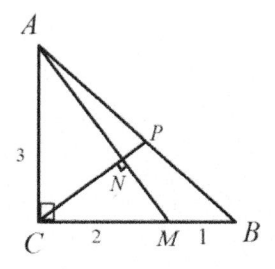

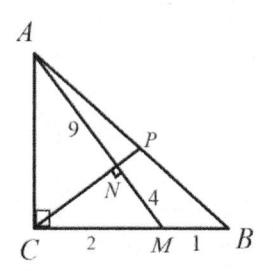

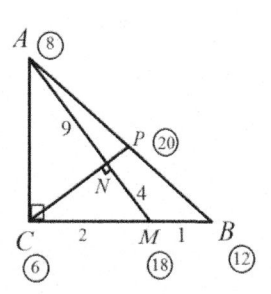

94

The Mass Points Method   **Chapter 5. Length and Area Problems**

$$\frac{AP}{PB} = \frac{m_B}{m_A} = \frac{12}{8} = \frac{3}{2}.$$

Example 17. In the figure, CD, AE, and BF are $\dfrac{2}{n-2}$ of their respective sides of triangle ABC and the area of triangle $N_1N_2N_3$ is $\dfrac{1}{7}S_{\triangle ABC}$. Find the greatest possible value of n.

(A) 5   (B) 6   (C) 7   (D) 8   (E) none of these

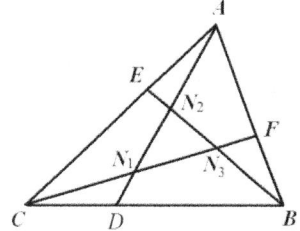

Solution: (B).

We know that $\dfrac{S_{\triangle ACD}}{S_{\triangle ABC}} = \dfrac{CD}{CB} = \dfrac{2}{n} \quad \Rightarrow \quad S_{\triangle ACD} = \dfrac{2}{n}S_{\triangle ABC}.$

We also know that $S_{\triangle ACN_1} = S_{\triangle BCN_3} = S_{\triangle ABN_2}.$

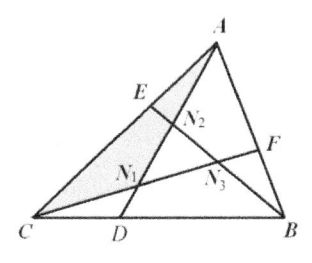

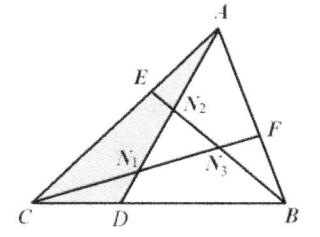

$$\frac{S_{\triangle ACN_1}}{S_{\triangle ACD}} = \frac{AN_1}{AD} = \frac{m_D}{m_{N_1}}$$

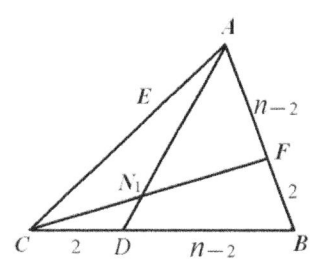

We remove the segment BE.
We label the length of each line segment as shown.
We assign a mass of 1 to point B.

$m_B \times (n-2) = m_C \times 2 \quad \Rightarrow \quad m_C = \dfrac{n-2}{2}.$

Similarly, we get $m_A = \dfrac{2}{n-2}$, $m_D = \dfrac{n}{2}$, and $m_{N_1} = \dfrac{n}{2} + \dfrac{2}{n-2} = \dfrac{n^2 - 2n + 4}{2(n-2)}.$

95

So $\dfrac{S_{\triangle ACN_1}}{S_{\triangle ACD}} = \dfrac{m_D}{m_{N_1}} = \dfrac{\frac{n}{2}}{\frac{n^2-2n+4}{2(n-2)}} = \dfrac{n(n-2)}{n^2-2n+4} \Rightarrow$

$S_{\triangle ACN_1} = \dfrac{n(n-2)}{n^2-2n+4} S_{\triangle ACD} = \dfrac{n(n-2)}{n^2-2n+4} \times \dfrac{2}{n} S_{\triangle ABC} = \dfrac{2(n-2)}{n^2-2n+4} S_{\triangle ABC}$

$S_{\triangle N_1 N_2 N_3} = S_{\triangle ABC} - (S_{\triangle ACN_1} + S_{\triangle BCN_3} + S_{\triangle ABN_2}) = S_{\triangle ABC} - 3 S_{\triangle ACN_1}$
$=$

$S_{\triangle ABC} - 3 \times \dfrac{2(n-2)}{n^2-2n+4} S_{\triangle ABC} = S_{\triangle ABC} - \dfrac{6(n-2)}{n^2-2n+4} S_{\triangle ABC}.$

We are also given that $S_{\triangle N_1 N_2 N_3} = \dfrac{1}{7} S_{\triangle ABC}$.

So $\dfrac{1}{7} S_{\triangle ABC} = S_{\triangle ABC} - \dfrac{6(n-2)}{n^2-2n+4} S_{\triangle ABC} \Rightarrow \dfrac{1}{7} = 1 - \dfrac{6(n-2)}{n^2-2n+4}$

$\Rightarrow \dfrac{6(n-2)}{n^2-2n+4} = \dfrac{6}{7} \Rightarrow \dfrac{n-2}{n^2-2n+4} = \dfrac{1}{7} \Rightarrow n^2 - 9n + 18 = 0$

$(n-3)(n-6) = 0 \Rightarrow n = 6.$

Example 18. (2017 State Sprint Round problem 29) Lines AB and DC are parallel, and transversals AC and BD intersect at a point X between the two lines so that $\dfrac{AX}{CX} = 5/7$. Points P and Q lie on segments AB and DC, respectively. The segment PQ intersects transversals BD and AC at points M and N, respectively, so that $PM = MN = NQ$. What is the ratio $\dfrac{AP}{BP}$? Express your answer as a common fraction.

The Mass Points Method   Chapter 5. Length and Area Problems

Solution: $\frac{2}{3}$.

Method 1 (official solution):
The description of the figure is a little hard to keep straight, so let's draw a diagram. For the sake of convenience I put D at the origin and A 3 units up (3 chosen because PQ is split into 3 congruent pieces—ratios are important, not magnitudes, so pick easy-to-work-with magnitudes; also, horizontal shearing has no impact on the result, so choose simplest values). $AB:CD = AX:CX = 5:7$, so let AB have length 5 and CD length 7. Since the y-component of Q and P is 0 and 3, respectively, to make the sub-segments congruent, the y-component of N and M must be 1 and 2, respectively. The line through AC has equation $y = 3 - 3/7\ x$, and the line through DB has equation $y = 3/5\ x$. $1 = 3 - 3/7\ x$ for point N, so the x-component of N is $14/3$; $2 = 3/5\ x$ for point M, so the x-component of M is $10/3$. Going from N to M decreased the x-component by $4/3$; going from M to P will decrease the x-component by another $4/3$, so the x-component of P is $10/3 - 4/3 = 2$ and AP has length 2 and PB has length $5 - 2 = 3$. Therefore, the ration $AB:BP = 2/3$. 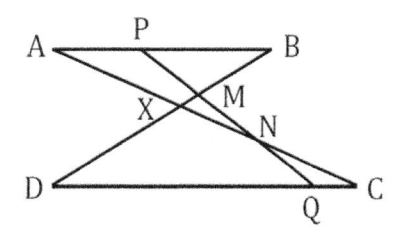
Note: There is a typo in the official solution: the last equation should be AP:BP = 2/3.

Method 2 (Mass Point Method):
We connect BN. We are applying the mass point method to triangle ABN.
Since $AB \parallel DC$, $\triangle ANP \sim \triangle CNQ$.

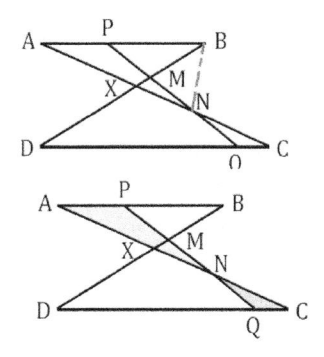

Thus we have $\dfrac{AN}{NC} = \dfrac{PN}{NQ} = \dfrac{1}{2}$ (1)

We are given that $\dfrac{AX}{CX} = \dfrac{5}{7}$ (2)

97

The Mass Points Method **Chapter 5. Length and Area Problems**

Since $CX = XN + NC$, we solve the system of equations (1) and (2) to get
$$\frac{AX}{XN} = \frac{5}{3}$$

We want to find $\frac{AP}{BP} = \frac{m_B}{m_A}$.

We label each line segment:

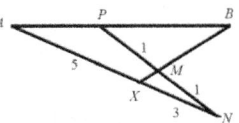

We assign $m_N = 5$, then we get $m_A = 3$, and $m_P = 5$.
So $m_B = 2$.

The answer is then $\frac{AP}{BP} = \frac{m_B}{m_A} = \frac{2}{3}$.

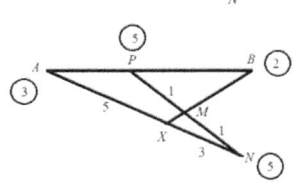

Method 3 (Similar triangle method):
We focus on three pairs of similar triangles as shown.

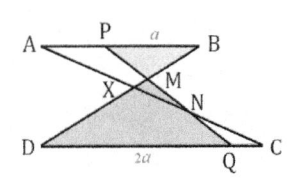

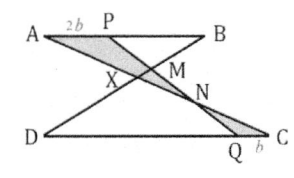

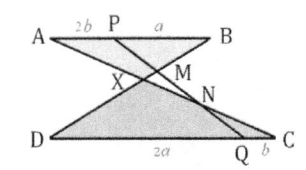

Since $AB \parallel DC$, $\triangle OMB \sim \triangle QMD$. Thus we have $\frac{PB}{DQ} = \frac{PM}{MQ} = \frac{1}{2}$.

So we let $PB = a$ and $DQ = 2a$.

Since $AB \parallel DC$, $\triangle ANP \sim \triangle CNQ$. Thus we have $\frac{AP}{QC} = \frac{PN}{NQ} = \frac{1}{2}$.

So we let $AP = 2b$ and $QC = b$.

Since $AB \parallel DC$, $\triangle AXB \sim \triangle CXD$. Thus we have $\frac{AB}{CD} = \frac{AX}{XC} = \frac{5}{7}$.

(1)

98

Or $\dfrac{2b+a}{2a+b} = \dfrac{5}{7}$ $\Rightarrow$ $7(2b+a) = 5(2a+b)$ $\Rightarrow$ $a = 3b$.

Thus $\dfrac{AP}{BP} = \dfrac{2b}{a} = \dfrac{2b}{3b} = \dfrac{2}{3}$.

Example 19. (2002 AIME II) In triangle *ABC*, point *D* is on *BC* with *CD* = 2 and *DB* = 5, point *E* is on *AC* with *CE* = 1 and *EA* = 3, *AB* = 8, and *AD* and *BE* intersect at *P*. Points *Q* and *R* lie on *AB* so that *PQ* is parallel to *CA* and *PR* is parallel to *CB*. It is given that the ratio of the area of triangle *PQR* to the area of triangle *ABC* is *m/n*, where *m* and *n* are relatively prime positive integers. Find *m* + *n*.

Solution: 901.
Method 1:
Since triangles *PQR* and *CAB* are similar, the ratio of their areas is

$$\dfrac{S_{\triangle PQR}}{S_{\triangle ABC}} = \left(\dfrac{RP}{BC}\right)^2 = \left(\dfrac{RP}{BD} \times \dfrac{BD}{BC}\right)^2 = \left(\dfrac{RP}{BD} \times \dfrac{5}{7}\right)^2 = \dfrac{25}{49}\left(\dfrac{RP}{BD}\right)^2 \qquad (1)$$

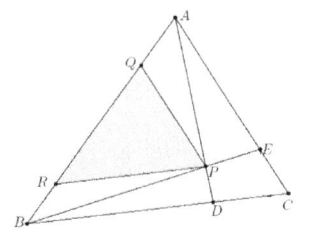

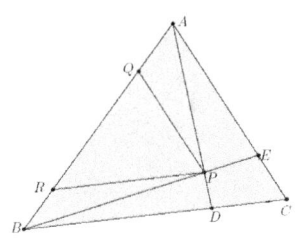

Triangles *RPA* and *BDA* are similar.

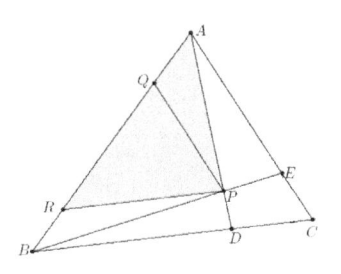

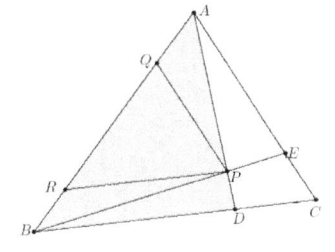

99

The Mass Points Method   **Chapter 5. Length and Area Problems**

It follows that $\dfrac{RP}{BD} = \dfrac{AP}{AD}$ (2)

Substituting (2) into (1): $\dfrac{S_{\triangle PQR}}{S_{\triangle ABC}} = \dfrac{25}{49}(\dfrac{AP}{AD})^2 = \dfrac{25}{49}(\dfrac{m_D}{m_P})^2$ (3)

Now we label each line segment as shown.

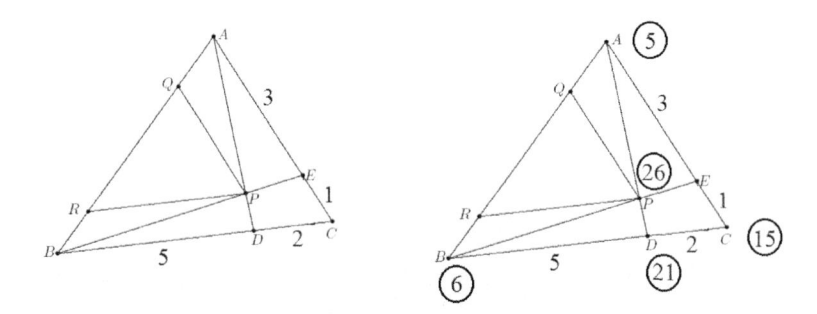

We assign $m_C = 15$. We get $m_B = 6$, $m_D = 21$, $m_A = 5$. Then $m_P = 26$.

Then $\dfrac{S_{\triangle PQR}}{S_{\triangle ABC}} = \dfrac{25}{49}(\dfrac{AP}{BD})^2 = \dfrac{25}{49}(\dfrac{m_D}{m_P})^2$

$= \dfrac{25}{49}(\dfrac{21}{26})^2 = \dfrac{225}{676}$.

Thus $m + n = 901$.

Method 2:
Since triangles PQR and CAB are similar, the ratio of their areas is
$\dfrac{S_{\triangle PQR}}{S_{\triangle ABC}} = (\dfrac{PQ}{AC})^2 = (\dfrac{PQ}{AE} \times \dfrac{AE}{AC})^2 = (\dfrac{PQ}{AE} \times \dfrac{3}{4})^2 = \dfrac{9}{16}(\dfrac{PQ}{AE})^2$ (1)

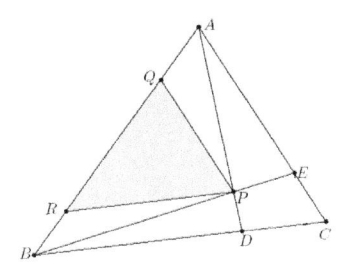

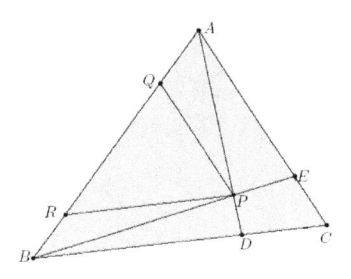

The Mass Points Method   **Chapter 5. Length and Area Problems**

Triangles *RPA* and *BDA* are similar.

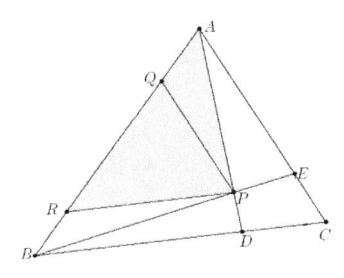

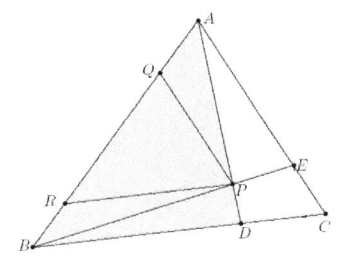

It follows that $\dfrac{PQ}{AE} = \dfrac{BP}{BE}$ (2)

Substituting (2) into (1): $\dfrac{S_{\triangle PQR}}{S_{\triangle ABC}} = \dfrac{9}{16}\left(\dfrac{BP}{BE}\right)^2 = \dfrac{9}{16}\left(\dfrac{m_E}{m_P}\right)^2$ (3)

Now we label each line segment as shown.

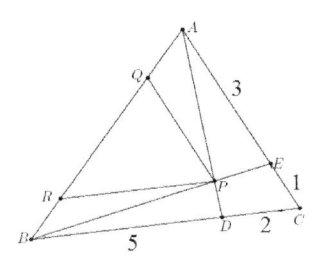

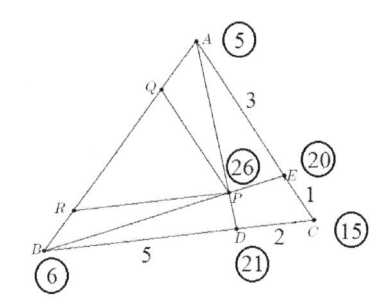

We assign $m_C = 15$. We get $m_B = 6$, $m_D = 21$, $m_A = 5$. Then $m_P = 26$. $m_E = 20$.

101

Then $\dfrac{S_{\triangle PQR}}{S_{\triangle ABC}} = \dfrac{9}{16}(\dfrac{BP}{BE})^2 = \dfrac{9}{16}(\dfrac{m_E}{m_P})^2$
$= \dfrac{9}{16}(\dfrac{20}{26})^2 = \dfrac{225}{676}$.
Thus $m + n = 901$.

This is the problem 13 in 2002 AIME II.

The Mass Points Method   Chapter 5. Length and Area Problems

Chapter 5. Problems

Problem 1. In triangle *ABC*, point *D* divides side *AC* so that $\frac{AD}{DC} = \frac{2}{3}$. Let *E* be the midpoint of *BD* and let *F* be the point of intersection of line *BC* and line *AE*. Given that the area of triangle *ABC* is 210, what is the area of triangle *BEF*?

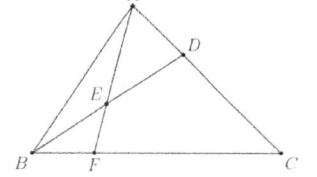

Problem 2. In triangle *ABC*, point *D* divides side *AC* so that $\frac{AD}{DC} = \frac{1}{2}$. Let *E* be the midpoint of *BD* and let *F* be the point of intersection of line *BC* and line *AE*. Given that the area of triangle *ABC* is 360, what is the area of triangle *AED*?

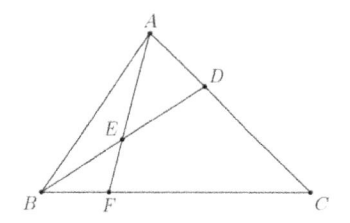

Problem 3. As shown in the figure on the right, $\triangle ABC$ is divided into six smaller triangles by lines drawn from the vertices through a common interior point. The areas of three triangles are as indicated. Find the area of $\triangle ABC$.

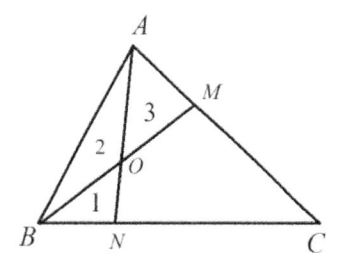

Problem 4. As shown in the figure, $\triangle ABC$ with the area of 40 is divided into three smaller triangles and one quadrilateral of the area *x*. If $\frac{AD}{DC} = \frac{2}{3}$ and $AE = BE$, find *x*.

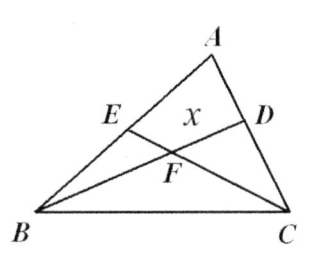

The Mass Points Method   Chapter 5. Length and Area Problems

Problem 5. As shown in the figure, $\triangle ABC$ is divided into three smaller triangles and one quadrilateral. If $\dfrac{BD}{DC} = \dfrac{2}{1}$, $\dfrac{CE}{EA} = \dfrac{1}{1}$, find $\dfrac{S_{\triangle ABF}}{S_{\triangle ABC}}$.

Express your answer as a common fraction.

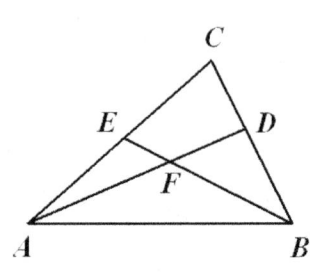

Problem 6. (2013 Mathcounts National Sprint 28) In right triangle ABC, shown here, $AC = 5$ units and $BC = 12$ units. Points D and E lie on AB and BC, respectively, so that CD is perpendicular to AB and E is the midpoint of BC. Segments AE and CD intersect at point F. What is the ratio of AF to FE? Express your answer as a common fraction.

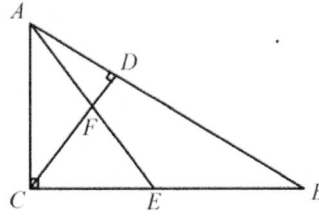

Problem 7. (AMC) In triangle ABC, $\angle CBA = 72°$, E is the midpoint of side AC, and D is a point on side BC such that $2BD = DC$; AD and BE intersect at F. The ratio of the area of $\triangle BDF$ to the area of quadrilateral $FDCE$ is

(A) $\dfrac{1}{5}$ (B) $\dfrac{1}{4}$ (C) $\dfrac{1}{3}$ (D) $\dfrac{2}{5}$ (E) none of these

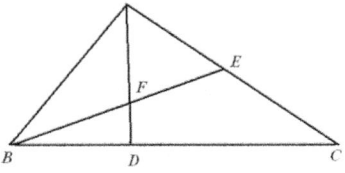

Problem 8. In square *ABCD*, two diagonals meet at *E*. The angle bisector of ∠*CBA* meets the diagonal *BD* at *G*. Find the length of *FD* if *GE* = 24.

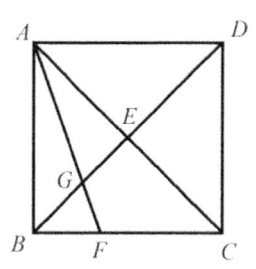

Problem 9. In △*ABC*, *E* is the midpoint of *AC*. Point *D* is on *BC* such that 2*BD* = *DC*. If *AD* and *BE* intersect at *F*, show that the area of quadrilateral *CEFD* is five times the area of triangle *BDF*.

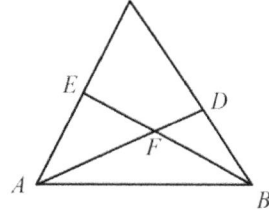

Problem 10. In △*ABC*, points *M* and *N* trisect the sides *AB*, and points *X* and *Y* trisect the sides *BC*. *AY* meets *BM* and *BN* at S and R, respectively. Find the ratio of the area of quadrilateral *CNRY* to the area of triangle *ABC*.

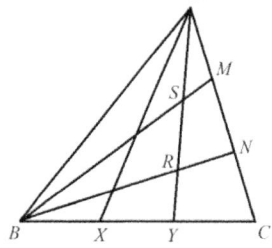

Problem 11. In triangle *ABC*, a point *D* is taken on *AB* and a point *E* is taken on *AC* such that *BD*: *DC* = 3 : 2, and *AE*: *EC* = 3 : 4. *AD* and *BE* intersect at *M*. Find the area of triangle *BMD* if the area of triangle *ABC* is 1.

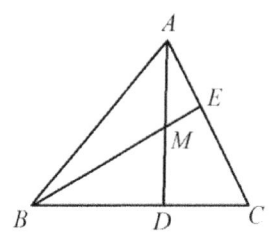

Problem 12. In triangle *ABC*, a point *D* is taken on *AB* and a point *E* is taken on *AC* such that *BD: DC* = 3 : 2, and *AE: EC* = 3 : 4. *AD* and *BE* intersect at *M*. Find the area of triangle *AEM* if the area of triangle *ABC* is 1.

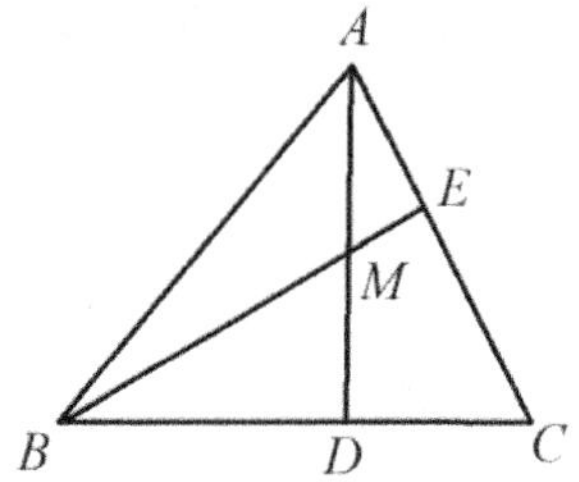

Problem 13. In triangle *ABC*, a point *D* is taken on *AB* and a point *E* is taken on *AC* such that *BD: DC* = 3 : 2, and *AE: EC* = 3 : 4. *AD* and *BE* intersect at *M*. Find the area of triangle *ABM* if the area of triangle *ABC* is 1.

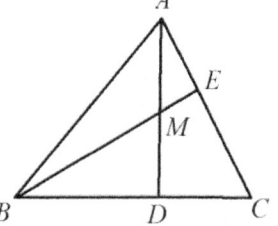

Problem 14. In triangle *ABC*, a point *D* is taken on *AB* and a point *E* is taken on *AC* such that *BD: DC* = 3 : 2, and *AE: EC* = 3 : 4. *AD* and *BE* intersect at *M*. Find the area of quadrilateral *CDME* if the area of triangle *ABC* is 1.

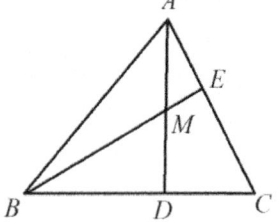

Problem 15. In the figure, *CD, AE*, and *BF* are one-third of their respective sides. Then the area of triangle $N_1N_2N_3$ is:

(A) $\frac{1}{10}S_{\triangle ABC}$ (B) $\frac{1}{9}S_{\triangle ABC}$ (C) $\frac{1}{7}S_{\triangle ABC}$ (D) $\frac{1}{6}S_{\triangle ABC}$
(E) none of these

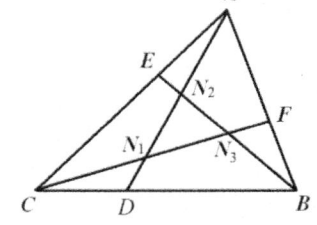

The Mass Points Method   **Chapter 5. Length and Area Problems**

Problem 16. In the figure, *CD, AE,* and *BF* are one-fourth of their respective sides. Then the area of triangle $N_1N_2N_3$ is:

(A) $\frac{1}{10}S_{\triangle ABC}$ (B) $\frac{1}{9}S_{\triangle ABC}$ (C) $\frac{1}{7}S_{\triangle ABC}$ (D) $\frac{4}{13}S_{\triangle ABC}$

(E) none of these

Problem 17. Isosceles right triangle *ABC* has $\angle C = 90°$. *M* is a point on *CB* such that *CM* = *MB*. *CP* $\perp$ *AB*. Find the value of $\frac{AP}{AB}$.

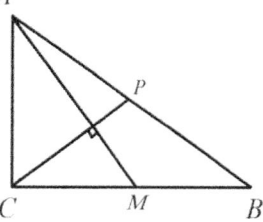

Problem 18. In right triangle *ABC*, shown here, *AC* = 5 units and *BC* = 12 units. Points *D* and *E* lie on *AB* and *BC* , respectively, so that *CD* is perpendicular to *AB* and *E* is the midpoint of *BC* . Segments *AE* and *CD* intersect at point *F*. What is the ratio of *AF* to *FE*? Express your answer as a common fraction.

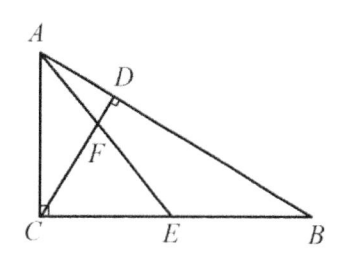

The Mass Points Method   Chapter 5. Length and Area Problems

Chapter 5. Solutions

Problem 1. Solution: 18.

Since $\dfrac{AD}{DC} = \dfrac{2}{3}$, $\dfrac{S_{\triangle ABD}}{S_{\triangle ABC}} = \dfrac{2}{5}$, $S_{\triangle ABD} = \dfrac{2}{5} S_{\triangle ABC} = 84$,

$S_{\triangle ABE} = \dfrac{1}{2} S_{\triangle ABD} = 42$.

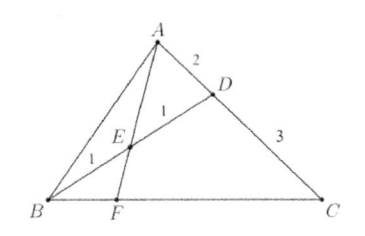

We assign 2 as the mass to point C.
Then we get $m_A = 3$, $m_D = 5$, $m_B = 5$, $m_F = 7$.

$\dfrac{S_{\triangle BEF}}{S_{\triangle ABE}} = \dfrac{EF}{EA} = \dfrac{m_A}{m_F} = \dfrac{3}{7}$ $\Rightarrow$

$S_{\triangle BEF} = \dfrac{3}{7} S_{\triangle ABE} = 18$.

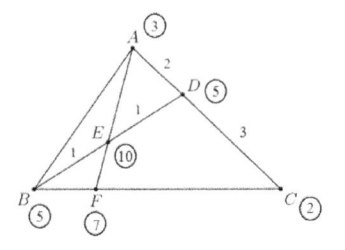

Problem 2. Solution: 30.

Since $\dfrac{AD}{DC} = \dfrac{1}{2}$, $\dfrac{S_{\triangle ABD}}{S_{\triangle ABC}} = \dfrac{1}{3}$, $S_{\triangle ABD} = \dfrac{1}{3} S_{\triangle ABC} = 120$,

$S_{\triangle ABE} = \dfrac{1}{2} S_{\triangle ABD} = 60$.

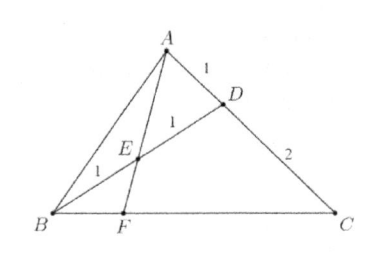

We assign 1 as the mass to point C.
Then we get $m_A = 2$, $m_D = 3$, $m_B = 3$, $m_F = 4$.

$\dfrac{S_{\triangle BEF}}{S_{\triangle ABE}} = \dfrac{EF}{EA} = \dfrac{m_A}{m_F} = \dfrac{2}{4} = \dfrac{1}{2}$ $\Rightarrow$

$S_{\triangle BEF} = \dfrac{1}{2} S_{\triangle ABE} = 30$.

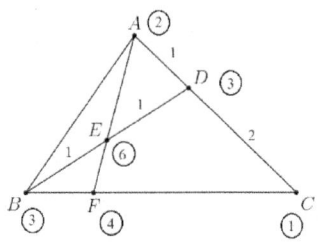

Problem 3. Solution: 30.

$\dfrac{S_{\triangle BAO}}{S_{\triangle MAO}} = \dfrac{2}{3} = \dfrac{BO}{OM}$.

108

$$\frac{S_{\Delta BAO}}{S_{\Delta BNO}} = \frac{2}{1} = \frac{AO}{ON}.$$

We label the length of each line segment as shown.

Let the masses in each point be m_A, m_B, m_C, m_M and m_O, respectively.

We assign a mass of 9 to point B.

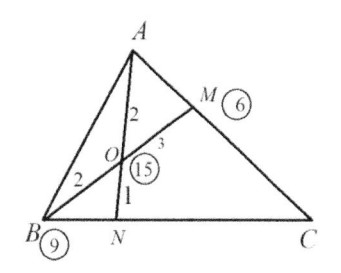

We look at the line segment BM.

$m_B \times 2 = m_M \times 3$

$\Rightarrow \quad m_M = 6$.

$m_O = m_B + m_M = 9 + 6 = 15$.

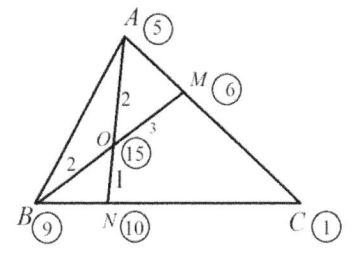

Next, we look at the line segment AN.

$m_A \times 2 = m_N \times 1$ with

$\Rightarrow \quad m_A + m_N = 15$.

It follows that $m_M = 5$ and $m_C = 6 - 5 = 1$.

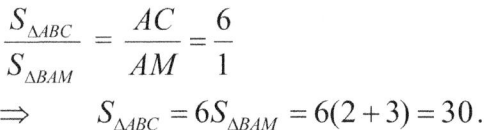

$\dfrac{AM}{CM} = \dfrac{5}{1}$. So $\dfrac{AC}{AM} = \dfrac{6}{1}$.

$\dfrac{S_{\Delta ABC}}{S_{\Delta BAM}} = \dfrac{AC}{AM} = \dfrac{6}{1}$

$\Rightarrow \quad S_{\Delta ABC} = 6 S_{\Delta BAM} = 6(2+3) = 30$.

Problem 4. Solution: 11.

We label the length of each line segment as shown.

We assign a mass of 3 to point A.

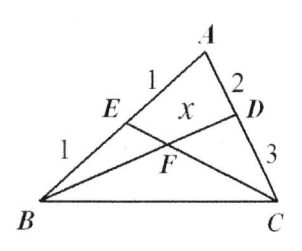

$m_A \times 2 = m_C \times 3$

$\Rightarrow \quad m_C = 2$ and $m_D = m_A + m_C = 3 + 2 = 5$.

Since $AE = BE$, $m_B = 2$.

Next, we look at the line segment BD:

$m_B \times BF = m_D \times FD$

$\Rightarrow \dfrac{FD}{BF} = \dfrac{3}{5}$

$\Rightarrow \dfrac{FD}{BD} = \dfrac{3}{8}.$

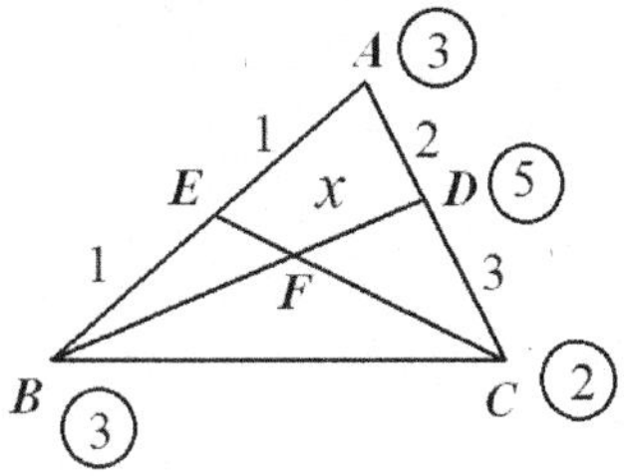

$\dfrac{S_{\triangle CDF}}{S_{\triangle CDB}} = \dfrac{FD}{BD} = \dfrac{3}{8}$

$\Rightarrow S_{\triangle CDF} = \dfrac{3}{8} S_{\triangle CDB} = \dfrac{3}{8} \times \dfrac{3}{5} S_{\triangle ABC} = 9.$

$S_{\triangle ACE} = \dfrac{1}{2} S_{\triangle ABC} = \dfrac{1}{2} \times 40 = 20.$

$\Rightarrow x = S_{\triangle ACE} - S_{\triangle CDF} = 20 - 9 = 11.$

Problem 5. Solution: $\dfrac{2}{5}.$

Let $\dfrac{BD}{DC} = \dfrac{m}{1}$, $\dfrac{CE}{EA} = \dfrac{n}{1}.$

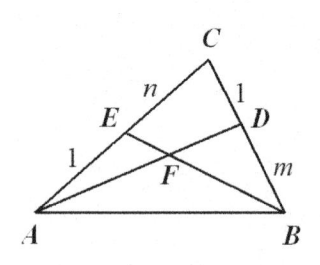

We label the length of each line segment as shown.
Connect CF and extend it to meet AB at G.
We assign a mass of 1 to point B.

$m_B \times m = m_C \times 1$

$\Rightarrow m_C = m.$

Next, we look at the line segment AC.

$m_C \times n = m_A \times 1 \qquad \Rightarrow \qquad m_A = mn \quad (1)$

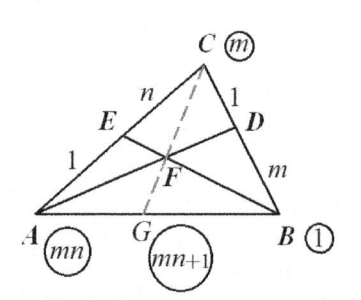

The Mass Points Method **Chapter 5. Length and Area Problems**

Next, we look at the line segment AB. Since F is the center mass of ABC, G is the center of mass of A and B. Therefore,
$m_G = m_A + m_B = mn + 1$.
$$\frac{S_{\triangle ABF}}{S_{\triangle ABC}} = \frac{FG}{CG} = \frac{m}{mn+1+m} = \frac{2}{2 \times 1 + 1 + 2} = \frac{2}{5}.$$

Problem 6. Solution: 25/72.
Method 1:
Triangle ABC is a 5-12-13 right triangle, so $AB = 13$.
We can determine from similar triangles
$AD = \dfrac{25}{13}$ and $DB = \dfrac{144}{13}$.
This gives us
$AD : DB = 25 : 144$, $CE : EB = 1 : 1$.

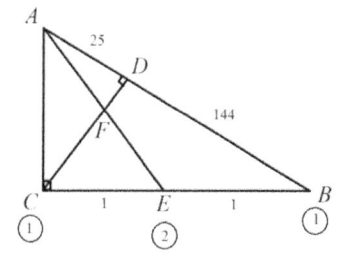

We label the line segments as shown below and then assign the mass 25 to B.
Thus $m_C = 25$, $m_E = 50$, and $m_A = 144$.
$$\frac{AE}{FE} = \frac{50}{144} = \frac{25}{72}.$$

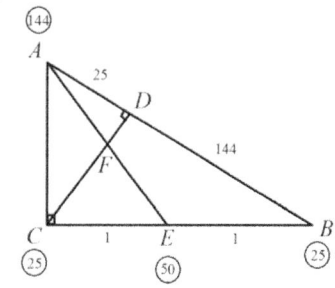

Method 2:
Triangle ABC is a 5-12-13 right triangle, so $AB = 13$.

We can determine from similar triangles
$AD = \dfrac{25}{13}$ and $DB = \dfrac{144}{13}$.
Draw $EG \parallel FD$.
Since $CE = EB$, $DG = BG = \dfrac{1}{2} \times \dfrac{144}{13} = \dfrac{72}{13}$.

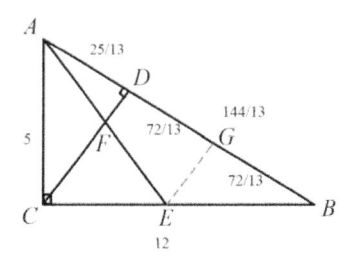

111

The Mass Points Method   Chapter 5. Length and Area Problems

Since triangle *AFD* is similar to triangle *AEC*,

$$\frac{AF}{FE} = \frac{AD}{DG} = \frac{\frac{25}{13}}{\frac{72}{13}} = \frac{25}{72}.$$

Problem 7. Solution: (A).
(1) We label the length of each line segment as shown.
Let the masses in each point be m_A, m_B, m_C, m_D, m_E, and m_F, respectively.

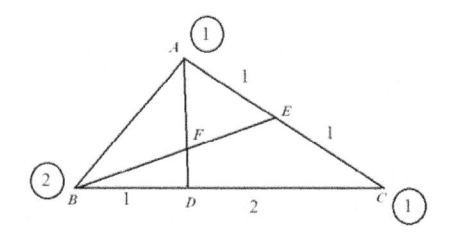

(2) We assign a mass of 2 to point *B*.
It follows that $m_C = 1$, $m_A = 1$.
(3) We then get $m_D = 1+2 = 3$, $m_E = 1+1 = 2$, and $m_F = 1+3 = 4$.

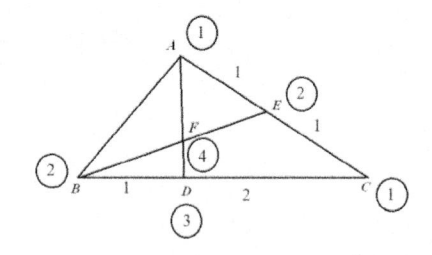

(4) Thus $\dfrac{S_{\triangle ABF}}{S_{\triangle AEF}} = \dfrac{BF}{EF} = \dfrac{m_E}{m_F} = 1$

$\Rightarrow S_{\triangle ABF} = S_{\triangle AEF}$

$\dfrac{S_{\triangle ABF}}{S_{\triangle DBF}} = \dfrac{AF}{DF} = \dfrac{m_D}{m_A} = 3 \Rightarrow S_{\triangle ABF} = 3S_{\triangle DBF}$

And $S_{\triangle ABE} = 6S_{\triangle DBF}$

Since $\dfrac{S_{\triangle ABF}}{S_{\triangle CBF}} = \dfrac{AE}{EC} = 1$

$\Rightarrow S_{\triangle ABF} = S_{\triangle CBF} = 6S_{\triangle DBF}$.

That is $S_{\triangle BDF} + S_{FDCE} = 6S_{\triangle DBF}$

$\Rightarrow \quad S_{FDCE} = 5S_{\triangle DBF}$

The ratio of the area of $\triangle BDF$ to the area of quadrilateral *FDCE* is then $\dfrac{1}{5}$.

Problem 8. Solution: 48.

112

Method 1:
By the Angle Bisector theorem, we have $\dfrac{AB}{BG} = \dfrac{AE}{GE}$

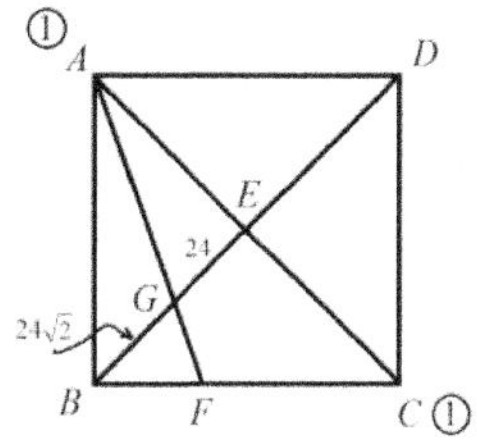

$\Rightarrow \quad \dfrac{AB}{BG} = \dfrac{\frac{\sqrt{2}}{2}AB}{24}$

$\Rightarrow \quad BG = 24\sqrt{2}$

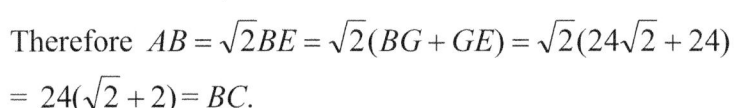

Therefore $AB = \sqrt{2}BE = \sqrt{2}(BG + GE) = \sqrt{2}(24\sqrt{2} + 24)$
$= 24(\sqrt{2} + 2) = BC$.

Let the masses in each point be m_A, m_B, m_C, and m_E, respectively.

We assign a mass of 1 to point A.
We get $m_C = 1$, $m_E = 2$, and
$m_B = \sqrt{2}$.

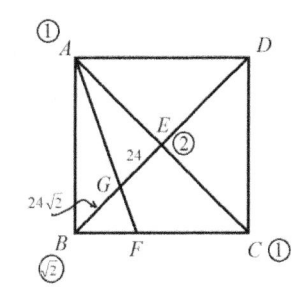

Thus $\dfrac{BF}{CF} = \dfrac{1}{\sqrt{2}} \Rightarrow BF = \dfrac{\sqrt{2}}{2}CF$.

$BC = BF + CF = 24(\sqrt{2} + 2) \Rightarrow$

$\dfrac{\sqrt{2}}{2}CF + CF = 24(\sqrt{2} + 2) \Rightarrow CF = 48$.

Method 2:
Draw $FH \parallel BD$. Then $FH \perp AC$.
Since $\angle CBF = \angle BAF$, $\angle ABF = \angle AHF = 90°$, and $AF = AF$, $\triangle ABF$ is congruent to $\triangle AHF$.

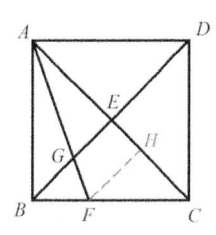

Thus $AB = AH$, $BF = FH$.
Let $BF = x$. It follows that $HC = FH = x$, $FC = \sqrt{2}\,x$,

$DC = (1+\sqrt{2})x$, $AC = (2+\sqrt{2})x$, and $AE = \dfrac{2+\sqrt{2}}{2}x$.

Since $FH \parallel BD$, $\dfrac{GE}{FH} = \dfrac{AE}{AH}$

$\Rightarrow \dfrac{24}{x} = \dfrac{\dfrac{2+\sqrt{2}}{2}x}{(2+\sqrt{2})x - x}$

Solving for x: $x = 24\sqrt{2}$.
The answer is $FC = \sqrt{2}\ x = 48$.

Method 3:
Draw $CK \parallel BD$ to meet the extension of AF at K. It follows that $CK = 2HGE = 48$.

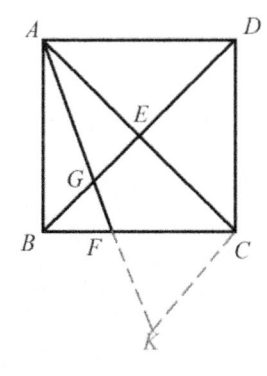

Since $\angle KAC = 22.5°$ and $\angle ACK = \angle AEG = 90°$, then $\angle K = 67.5°$.
Since $\angle FCK = 45°$, then $\angle CFK = 180° - \angle FCK - \angle K = 67.5°$.
Thus triangle CFK is an isosceles triangle with $FC = CK$.
The answer is $FC = 48$.

Problem 9. Solution:

First we label the line segments as shown:

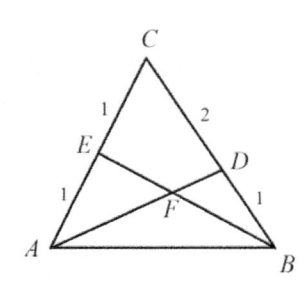

Next, we assign the mass: $m_A = 1$.
It follows that $m_C = 1$, $m_C = 1$, $m_E = 2$.
$m_B = 2$, $m_D = 3$, $m_F = 4$.

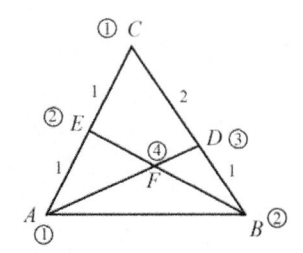

$\dfrac{S_{\triangle BDF}}{S_{\triangle BDA}} = \dfrac{DF}{AD} = \dfrac{m_A}{m_F} = \dfrac{1}{4}$

$\Rightarrow S_{\triangle BDF} = \dfrac{1}{4}S_{\triangle BDA} = \dfrac{1}{4} \times \dfrac{1}{3}S_{\triangle ABC} = \dfrac{1}{12}S_{\triangle ABC}$ \hfill (1)

The Mass Points Method   **Chapter 5. Length and Area Problems**

$$\frac{S_{\triangle AEF}}{S_{\triangle AEB}} = \frac{EF}{EB} = \frac{m_B}{m_F} = \frac{2}{4} = \frac{1}{2}$$

$$\Rightarrow S_{\triangle AEF} = \frac{1}{2} S_{\triangle AEB} = \frac{1}{2} \times \frac{1}{2} S_{\triangle ABC} = \frac{1}{4} S_{\triangle ABC}.$$

$$S_{EFDC} = S_{\triangle ACD} - S_{\triangle AEF} = \frac{2}{3} S_{\triangle ABC} - \frac{1}{4} S_{\triangle ABC} = \frac{5}{12} S_{\triangle ABC} \quad (2)$$

$$(2) \div (1): \frac{S_{EFDC}}{S_{\triangle BDF}} = \frac{\frac{5}{12} S_{\triangle ABC}}{\frac{1}{12} S_{\triangle ABC}} = 5$$

$$\Rightarrow S_{EFDC} = 5 S_{\triangle BDF}.$$

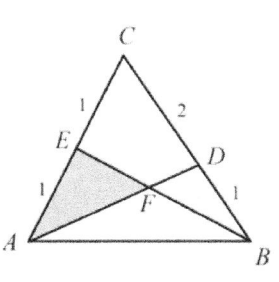

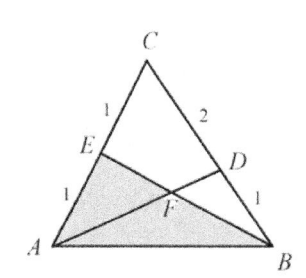

Problem 10. Solution: $\frac{5}{42}$.

$$S_{\triangle ACY} = \frac{1}{3} S_{\triangle ABC}$$

$$S_{\triangle ABN} = \frac{2}{3} S_{\triangle ABC}$$

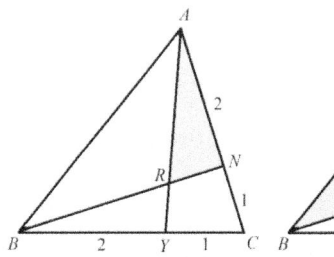

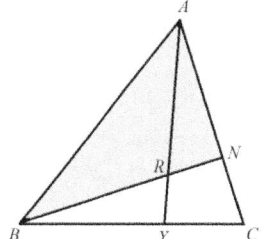

We remove the line segments AX and BM, and label the line segments.
Then we assign the mass $m_B = 1$.
It follows that $m_C = 2$, $m_A = 1$, $m_N = 5$.
$m_R = 4$.

$$\frac{S_{\triangle ANR}}{S_{\triangle ABN}} = \frac{RN}{BN} = \frac{m_B}{m_R} = \frac{1}{4}$$

$$\Rightarrow S_{\triangle ANR} = \frac{1}{4} S_{\triangle ABN} = \frac{1}{4} \times \frac{2}{3} S_{\triangle ABC} = \frac{1}{6} S_{\triangle ABC} \quad (1)$$

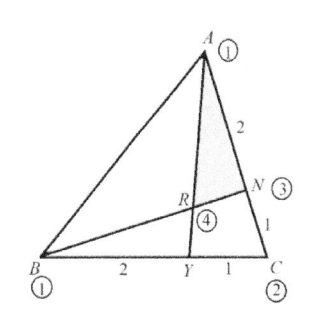

115

The Mass Points Method   **Chapter 5. Length and Area Problems**

$S_{CNRY} = S_{\triangle ACY} - S_{\triangle ANR} = \frac{1}{3}S_{\triangle ABC} - \frac{1}{6}S_{\triangle ABC} = \frac{1}{6}S_{\triangle ABC}$.

Therefore, $\frac{S_{CNRY}}{S_{\triangle ABC}} = \frac{1}{6}$.

Problem 11. Solution: $\frac{4}{15}$.

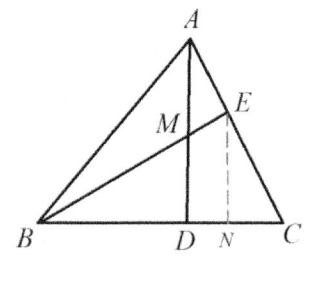

Method 1:
Draw $EN // AD$ to meet BC at N.
Since $BD : DC = 3 : 2$ and $AE : EC = 3 : 4$, $NC : DN : BD = 8 : 6 : 21$.

We know that $S_{\triangle BCE} = \frac{4}{7}S_{\triangle ABC} = \frac{4}{7}$. Thus

$S_{\triangle BNE} = \frac{27}{35}S_{\triangle BEC} = \frac{27 \times 4}{35 \times 7}$.

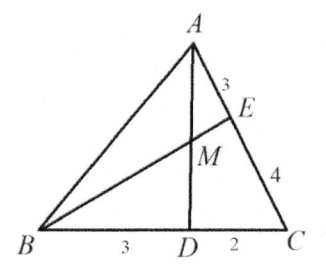

Since $DM // EN$, $\triangle BDM \sim \triangle BNE$. Then

$S_{\triangle BDM} = (\frac{21}{27})^2 S_{\triangle BNC} = \frac{49}{81} \times \frac{27 \times 4}{35 \times 7} = \frac{4}{15}$.

Method 2:
We know that $\frac{S_{\triangle ABD}}{S_{\triangle ABC}} = \frac{BD}{BC} = \frac{3}{5}$

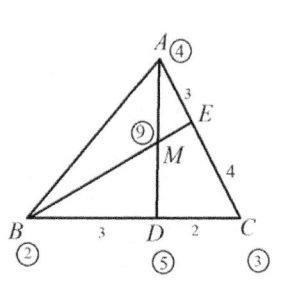

$S_{\triangle ABD} = \frac{3}{5}S_{\triangle ABC} = \frac{3}{5}$

We label each line segment as shown.
We assign $m_B = 2$.
It follows that $m_C = 3$, $m_A = 4$, $m_D = 5$, and $m_M = 9$.

$\frac{S_{\triangle BMD}}{S_{\triangle ABD}} = \frac{BD}{DA} = \frac{m_A}{m_M} = \frac{4}{9}$

$S_{\triangle BMD} = \frac{4}{9}S_{\triangle ABD} = \frac{4}{9} \times \frac{3}{5} = \frac{4}{15}$

The Mass Points Method   Chapter 5. Length and Area Problems

Problem 12. Solution: $\dfrac{2}{21}$.

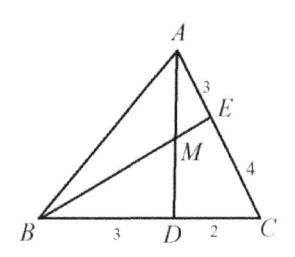

We know that $\dfrac{S_{\triangle ABE}}{S_{\triangle ABC}} = \dfrac{AE}{AC} = \dfrac{3}{7}$

$S_{\triangle ABE} = \dfrac{3}{7} S_{\triangle ABC} = \dfrac{3}{7}$

We label each line segment as shown and assign $m_B = 2$. It follows that
$m_C = 3$, $m_A = 4$, $m_E = 7$, and $m_M = 9$.

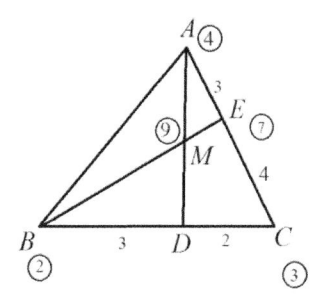

$\dfrac{S_{\triangle AEM}}{S_{\triangle ABE}} = \dfrac{EM}{BE} = \dfrac{m_B}{m_M} = \dfrac{2}{9}$

$S_{\triangle AEM} = \dfrac{2}{9} S_{\triangle ABE} = \dfrac{2}{9} \times \dfrac{3}{7} = \dfrac{2}{21}$.

Problem 13. Solution: $\dfrac{1}{3}$.

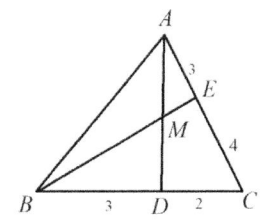

We know that $\dfrac{S_{\triangle ABD}}{S_{\triangle ABC}} = \dfrac{BD}{BC} = \dfrac{3}{5}$

$S_{\triangle ABD} = \dfrac{3}{5} S_{\triangle ABC} = \dfrac{3}{5}$

We label each line segment as shown and assign
$m_B = 2$. It follows that $m_C = 3$, $m_A = 4$, $m_D = 5$, and $m_M = 9$.

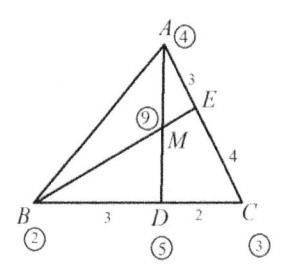

$\dfrac{S_{\triangle ABM}}{S_{\triangle ABD}} = \dfrac{AM}{AD} = \dfrac{m_D}{m_M} = \dfrac{5}{9}$

$S_{\triangle ABM} = \dfrac{4}{9} S_{\triangle ABD} = \dfrac{5}{9} \times \dfrac{3}{5} = \dfrac{1}{3}$.

Problem 14. Solution: $\dfrac{32}{105}$.

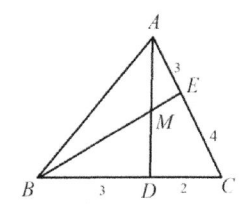

We know that $\dfrac{S_{\triangle ABE}}{S_{\triangle ABC}} = \dfrac{AE}{AC} = \dfrac{3}{7}$

$S_{\triangle ABE} = \dfrac{3}{7} S_{\triangle ABC} = \dfrac{3}{7}$

We label each line segment as shown and assign $m_B = 2$. It follows that $m_C = 3$, $m_A = 4$, $m_E = 7$, and $m_M = 9$.

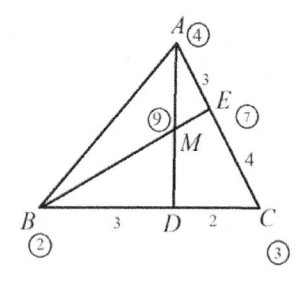

$\dfrac{S_{\triangle AEM}}{S_{\triangle ABE}} = \dfrac{EM}{BE} = \dfrac{m_B}{m_M} = \dfrac{2}{9}$

$S_{\triangle AEM} = \dfrac{2}{9} S_{\triangle ABE} = \dfrac{2}{9} \times \dfrac{3}{7} = \dfrac{2}{21}$.

We also know that $\dfrac{S_{\triangle ACD}}{S_{\triangle ABC}} = \dfrac{CD}{BC} = \dfrac{2}{5}$. Thus, $S_{\triangle ACD} = \dfrac{2}{5}$.

$S_{CEMD} = S_{\triangle ACD} - S_{\triangle AEM} = \dfrac{2}{5} - \dfrac{2}{21} = \dfrac{32}{105}$.

Problem 15. Solution: (C).

We know that $\dfrac{S_{\triangle ACD}}{S_{\triangle ABC}} = \dfrac{CD}{CB} = \dfrac{1}{3}$ $\Rightarrow$ $S_{\triangle ACD} = \dfrac{1}{3} S_{\triangle ABC}$.

We also know that $S_{\triangle ACN_1} = S_{\triangle BCN_3} = S_{\triangle ABN_2}$.

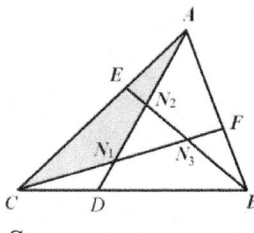

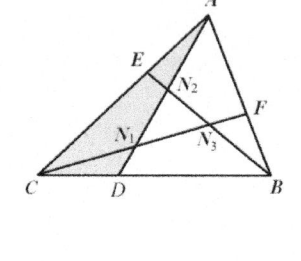

$\dfrac{S_{\triangle ACN_1}}{S_{\triangle ACD}} = \dfrac{AN_1}{AD} = \dfrac{m_D}{m_{N_1}}$

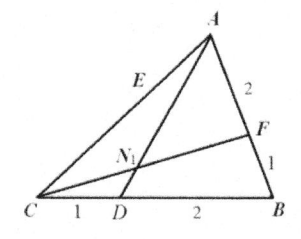

We remove the segment BE, label the length of each line segment, and assign a mass of 2 to point B.

118

The Mass Points Method **Chapter 5. Length and Area Problems**

$m_B \times 2 = m_C \times 1 \quad \Rightarrow \quad m_C = 4$.

Similarly we get $m_A = 1$, $m_D = 6$, and $m_{N_1} = 7$

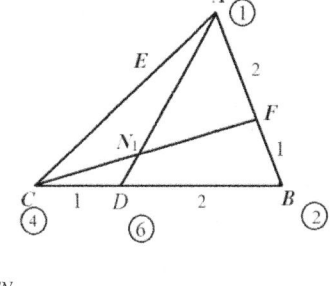

So $\dfrac{S_{\triangle ACN_1}}{S_{\triangle ACD}} = \dfrac{m_D}{m_{N_1}} = \dfrac{6}{7} \Rightarrow$

$S_{\triangle ACN_1} = \dfrac{6}{7} S_{\triangle ACD} = \dfrac{6}{7} \times \dfrac{1}{3} S_{\triangle ABC} = \dfrac{2}{7} S_{\triangle ABC}$

$S_{\triangle N_1 N_2 N_3} = S_{\triangle ABC} - (S_{\triangle ACN_1} + S_{\triangle BCN_3} + S_{\triangle ABN_2}) = S_{\triangle ABC} - 3 S_{\triangle ACN_1}$

$= S_{\triangle ABC} - 3 \times \dfrac{2}{7} S_{\triangle ABC} = \dfrac{1}{7} S_{\triangle ABC}$.

Problem 16. Solution: (D).

We know that $\dfrac{S_{\triangle ACD}}{S_{\triangle ABC}} = \dfrac{CD}{CB} = \dfrac{1}{4} \quad \Rightarrow \quad S_{\triangle ACD} = \dfrac{1}{4} S_{\triangle ABC}$.

We also know that $S_{\triangle ACN_1} = S_{\triangle BCN_3} = S_{\triangle ABN_2}$.

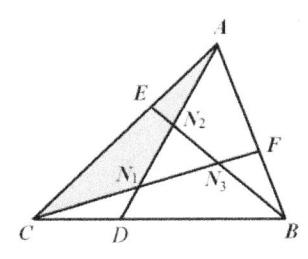

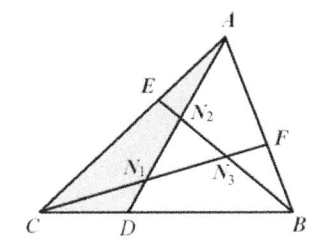

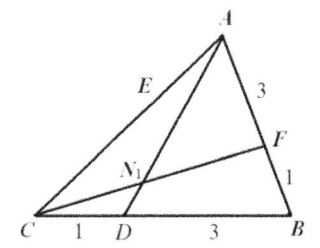

$\dfrac{S_{\triangle ACN_1}}{S_{\triangle ACD}} = \dfrac{AN_1}{AD} = \dfrac{m_D}{m_{N_1}}$

We remove the segment *BE*, label the length of each line segment as shown, and assign a mass of 3 to point *B*.

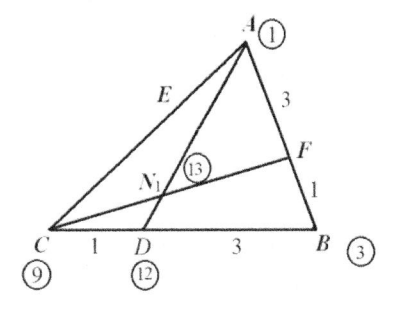

$m_B \times 3 = m_C \times 1 \quad \Rightarrow \quad m_C = 9$.

Similarly, we get $m_A = 1$, $m_D = 12$, and $m_{N_1} = 12$

119

The Mass Points Method   **Chapter 5. Length and Area Problems**

Thus, $\dfrac{S_{\triangle ACN_1}}{S_{\triangle ACD}} = \dfrac{m_D}{m_{N_1}} = \dfrac{12}{13} \Rightarrow S_{\triangle ACN_1} = \dfrac{12}{13} S_{\triangle ACD} = \dfrac{12}{13} \times \dfrac{1}{4} S_{\triangle ABC} = \dfrac{3}{13} S_{\triangle ABC}$

$S_{\triangle N_1 N_2 N_3} = S_{\triangle ABC} - (S_{\triangle ACN_1} + S_{\triangle BCN_3} + S_{\triangle ABN_2}) = S_{\triangle ABC} - 3 S_{\triangle ACN_1}$

$= S_{\triangle ABC} - 3 \times \dfrac{3}{13} S_{\triangle ABC} = \dfrac{4}{13} S_{\triangle ABC}$.

Problem 17. Solution: 2/3.

$\dfrac{AP}{AB} = \dfrac{m_B}{m_P}$.

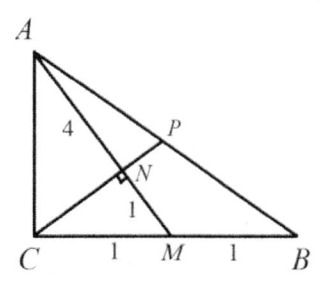

We know that $\dfrac{CM}{MB} = \dfrac{1}{1}$

$AM = \sqrt{2^2 + 1^2} = \sqrt{5}$

$CM^2 = AM \times MN \quad \Rightarrow \quad 1^2 = \sqrt{5} \times MN \Rightarrow MN = \dfrac{1}{\sqrt{5}}$.

$AC^2 = AM \times AN \quad \Rightarrow \quad 2^2 = \sqrt{5} \times AN \Rightarrow AN = \dfrac{4}{\sqrt{5}}$.

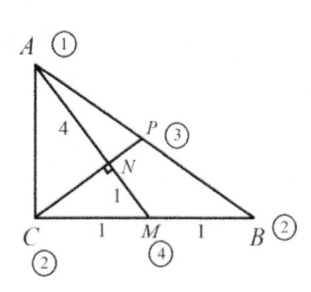

$\dfrac{AN}{MN} = \dfrac{\frac{4}{\sqrt{5}}}{\frac{1}{\sqrt{5}}} = \dfrac{4}{1}$.

We label each line segment as shown.

We assign $m_B = 2$. We get $m_C = 2$, $m_M = 4$, $m_A = 1$. Then $m_P = 3$. $\dfrac{AP}{AB} = \dfrac{m_B}{m_P} = \dfrac{2}{3}$.

Problem 18. Solution: $\dfrac{25}{72}$.

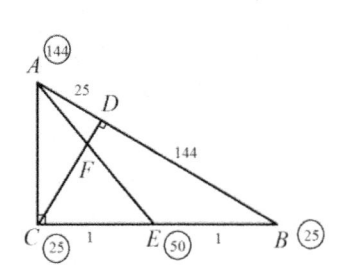

$\dfrac{AF}{FE} = \dfrac{m_E}{m_A}$.

Triangle ABC is $5 - 12 - 13$ right triangle.
So $AB = 13$.

120

$$AC^2 = AB \times AD \quad \Rightarrow \quad 5^2 = 13 \times AD \quad \Rightarrow AD = \frac{25}{13}$$

$$BC^2 = AB \times BD \quad \Rightarrow \quad 12^2 = 13 \times BD \quad \Rightarrow BD = \frac{144}{13}.$$

$$\frac{AD}{BD} = \frac{25}{144}.$$

We label the length of each line segment as shown.

Let the masses in each point be m_A, m_B, m_C, and m_E, respectively.

We assign a mass of 25 to point B. So we get $m_A = 144$, $m_C = 25$, and $m_E = 50$.

$$\frac{AF}{FE} = \frac{m_E}{m_A} = \frac{50}{144} = \frac{25}{72}.$$

The Mass Points Method Chapter 6. Quadrilaterals and Space Problems

Chapter 6. Quadrilaterals and Space Problems

Theorem 1. $ABCD$ is a parallelogram. Given m_A, m_B, m_C, m_D, the masses of three vertices A, B, C, and D, we have the following relationship:
$m_A + m_C = m_B + m_D$.

Proof:
We draw AC and BD, the diagonals of $ABCD$. AC and BD meet at point E.

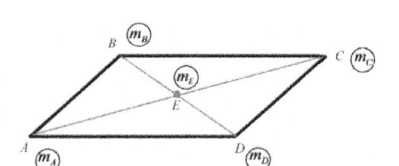

Now we look at the line segment AC. Since E is the midpoint of AC, we have
$m_E = m_A + m_C$

Now we look at the line segment BD. Since E is the midpoint of BD, we have
$m_E = m_B + m_D$.

Thus we have $m_A + m_C = m_B + m_D$

Theorem 2. Line segments AC and BD meet at point E. Given m_A, m_B, m_C, m_D, the masses of points A, B, C, and D, we have the following relationship:
$m_A + m_C = m_B + m_D$.

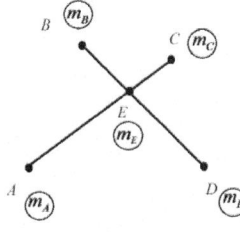

Proof:
E is the center of mass for line segment AC. So we have
$m_E = m_A + m_C$

E is also the center of mass for line segment BD. So we have
$m_E = m_B + m_D$.

Thus we have $m_A + m_C = m_B + m_D$

The Mass Points Method   Chapter 6. Quadrilaterals and Space Problems

Example 1. (2012 Mathcounts State Sprint 30) In rectangle $ABCD$, shown here, point M is the midpoint of side BC, and point N lies on CD such that $DN : NC = 1 : 4$. Segment BN intersects AM and AC at points R and S, respectively. If $NS : SR : RB = x : y : z$, where x, y and z are positive integers, what is the minimum possible value of $x + y + z$?

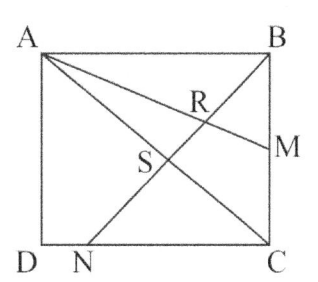

Solution: 126.

Since $AB // CD$, $\triangle ABS \sim \triangle CNS$.

Since $DN : NC = 1 : 4$, $NC = \dfrac{4}{5} AB$.

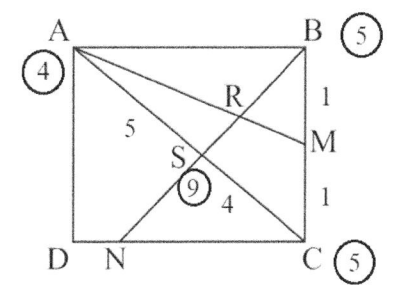

$\dfrac{AB}{NC} = \dfrac{BS}{NS} = \dfrac{AS}{SC} = \dfrac{5}{4} \quad \Rightarrow \quad \dfrac{y+z}{x} = \dfrac{5}{4}$

We assign the mass value of 5 to point C.
$m_C = 5$, $m_B = 5$, $m_A = 4$, $m_S = 9$.
Thus $y : z = SR/RB = 5 : 9$.
Since we only want to find the ratio, we let $y = 5$ and $z = 9$.
$(y + z)/x = 5/4 \quad \Rightarrow \quad x = 56/5$.
$x : y : z = 56/5 : 5 : 9 = 56/5 : 25/5 : 45/5$.
The minimum possible value of $x + y + z$ is $56 + 25 + 45 = 126$.

Example 2. In parallelogram $ABCD$, shown here, points E and F are the midpoints of sides AB and BC, respectively. AF meets DE at G and BD at H. Find the area of quadrilateral $BHGE$ if the area of $ABCD$ is 60.

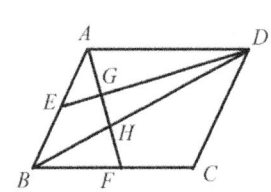

Solution: 7.
Since $ABCD$ is a parallelogram, $AD//BC$, triangle ADH is similar to triangle FBH.
$\dfrac{AD}{BF} = \dfrac{DH}{BH} = \dfrac{2}{1}$.
We label each line segment as shown.

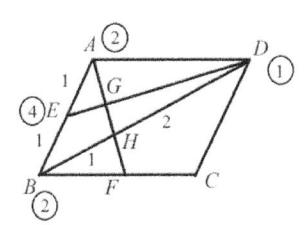

123

Then we assign the mass value of 2 to point B.
$m_D = 1$, $m_A = 2$, $m_E = 4$, $m_G = 5$, and $m_H = 3$.

$$\frac{S_{\triangle ABH}}{S_{\triangle ABD}} = \frac{BH}{BD} = \frac{m_D}{m_H} = \frac{1}{3} \quad \Rightarrow \quad S_{\triangle ABH} = \frac{1}{3} S_{\triangle ABD} = \frac{1}{6} S_{ABCD} = 10$$

$$\frac{S_{\triangle AEG}}{S_{\triangle AED}} = \frac{EG}{ED} = \frac{m_D}{m_G} = \frac{1}{5} \quad \Rightarrow \quad S_{\triangle AEG} = \frac{1}{5} S_{\triangle AED} = \frac{1}{20} S_{ABCD} = 3$$

Therefore $S_{BHGE} = S_{\triangle ABH} - S_{\triangle AEG} = 10 - 3 = 7$.

Example 3. In trapezoid $ABCD$, $AB = 3CD$ and $AB \parallel CD$. E is the midpoint of the diagonal AC. BE meets AD at F. Find the value of $AF : FD$. Express your answer as a common fraction.

Solution: $\frac{3}{2}$.

Extend CD and BF to meet at G. Since $CG \parallel AB$, $\triangle ABE \sim \triangle CGE$. So
$\frac{CG}{AB} = \frac{CE}{AE} = 1 \Rightarrow CG = AB \Rightarrow GD + CD = 3CD \Rightarrow$
$GD = 2CD$
We label each line segment as shown.
Then we assign the mass value of 2 to point A.
Then we calculate: $m_C = 2$, $m_G = 1$, $m_D = 3$.
$\frac{AF}{FD} = \frac{m_D}{m_A} = \frac{3}{2}$.

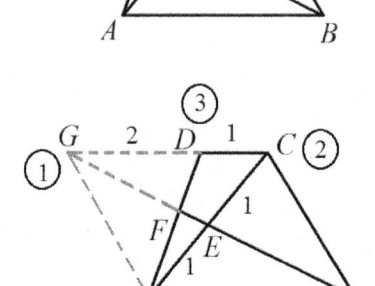

Example 4. (2018 AMC 10 A Problem 24) Triangle ABC with $AB = 50$ and $AC = 10$ has area 120. Let D be the midpoint of AB, and let E be the midpoint of AC.

The Mass Points Method   Chapter 6. Quadrilaterals and Space Problems

The angle bisector of BAC intersects DE and BC at F and G, respectively. What is the area of quadrilateral $FDBG$?

(A) 60   (B) 65   (C) 70   (D) 75   (E) 80

Solution: (D).

$$S_{\triangle AED} = \frac{1}{2} AE \times AD = \frac{1}{2} \times 5 \times 25 \sin(2\alpha) \quad (1)$$

$$S_{\triangle ACB} = \frac{1}{2} AC \times AB = \frac{1}{2} \times 10 \times 50 \sin(2\alpha) \quad (2)$$

(1) ÷ (2): $S_{\triangle AED} = \frac{1}{4} \times S_{\triangle ACB} = 30$

We label each line segment as shown.
Then we assign the mass value of 1 to point B. Then we calculate: $m_C = 5$, $m_G = 6$, $m_{A_{AB}} = 1$, $m_D = 2$, $m_{A_{AC}} = 5$, $m_E = 10$, $m_F = 12$, $m_{A_{AG}} = 6$.

$$\frac{S_{\triangle AFD}}{S_{\triangle AED}} = \frac{DF}{DE} = \frac{m_E}{m_F} = \frac{10}{12} = \frac{5}{6}$$

$$\Rightarrow \quad S_{\triangle AFD} = \frac{5}{6} \times 30 = 25 \ .$$

$$\frac{S_{\triangle ABG}}{S_{\triangle ABC}} = \frac{BG}{BC} = \frac{m_C}{m_G} = \frac{5}{6} \quad \Rightarrow \quad S_{\triangle ABG} = \frac{5}{6} \times 120 = 100$$

$$S_{FDBG} = S_{\triangle ABG} - S_{\triangle AFD} = 100 - 25 = 75 \ .$$

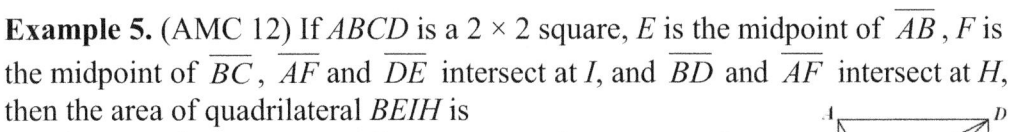

Example 5. (AMC 12) If $ABCD$ is a 2 × 2 square, E is the midpoint of $\overline{AB}$, F is the midpoint of $\overline{BC}$, $\overline{AF}$ and $\overline{DE}$ intersect at I, and $\overline{BD}$ and $\overline{AF}$ intersect at H, then the area of quadrilateral $BEIH$ is

(A) $\frac{1}{3}$ (B) $\frac{2}{5}$ (C) $\frac{7}{15}$ (D) $\frac{8}{15}$ (E) $\frac{3}{5}$

Solution: (C).

The Mass Points Method Chapter 6. Quadrilaterals and Space Problems

Since $\triangle ADH \sim \triangle FBH$, $\dfrac{DH}{BH} = \dfrac{AD}{BF} = \dfrac{1}{2}$.

We label each line segments and assign the value 1 to the point D and calculate the masses for each point as shown.

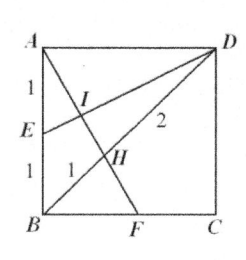

$\dfrac{S_{\triangle ABH}}{S_{\triangle ABD}} = \dfrac{BH}{BD} = \dfrac{1}{3}$

$\Rightarrow \quad S_{\triangle ABH} = \dfrac{1}{3} S_{\triangle ABD} = \dfrac{1}{3} \times \dfrac{2 \times 2}{2} = \dfrac{2}{3}$

$\dfrac{S_{\triangle AEI}}{S_{\triangle AED}} = \dfrac{EI}{ED} = \dfrac{m_D}{m_I} = \dfrac{1}{5}$

$\Rightarrow \quad S_{\triangle AEI} = \dfrac{1}{5} S_{\triangle AED} = \dfrac{1}{5} \times \dfrac{1 \times 2}{2} = \dfrac{1}{5}$.

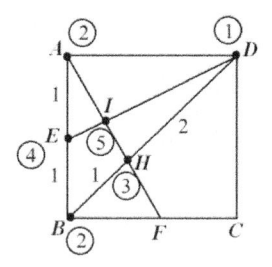

The answer is then $S_{BEIH} = S_{\triangle ABH} - S_{\triangle AEI} = \dfrac{2}{3} - \dfrac{1}{5} = \dfrac{7}{15}$.

Example 6. $ABCD$ is a trapezoid with $CD = 2AB$. Let E be in BC such that $BE : EC = 1 : 3$, F is the intersection of the diagonals. Extend EF to meet AD at G. Find $EF : FG$ and $AG : GD$.

Solution: 7 : 8 and 3 : 4.
Since $AB : DC = 1 : 2$, we have $BF : FD = AF : FC = 1 : 2$. So we can label each line segment and assign mass 2 to C.

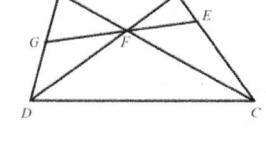

Then we get $m_A = 4$, $m_B = 6$, $m_D = 3$, $m_G = 7$, $m_E = 8$.
We then find $\dfrac{EF}{FG} = \dfrac{m_G}{m_E} = \dfrac{7}{8}$ and $\dfrac{AG}{GD} = \dfrac{m_D}{m_A} = \dfrac{3}{4}$.

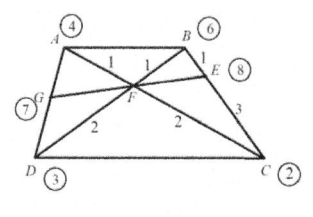

Example 7. In quadrilateral $ABCD$, E, F, G, H are the trisection points of AB, CB, CD, and AD, respectively as shown in the figure. Let EG intersect HF at K. Find the numerical values of $GK : KE$ and $HK : KF$.

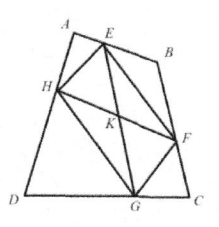

The Mass Points Method   Chapter 6. Quadrilaterals and Space Problems

Solution: 1 : 1 and 1 : 1.
We have $AH : HD = CF : FB = AE : EB = CG + GD = 1 : 2$.
So we can label each line segment and assign mass 2 to C.

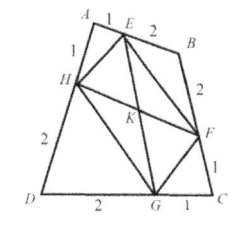

Then we get $m_B = 1$, $m_F = 3$, $m_A = 2$, $m_E = 3$, $m_D = 1$, $m_H = 3$.

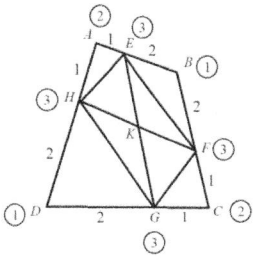

We then find $\dfrac{GK}{KE} = \dfrac{m_E}{m_G} = \dfrac{3}{3} = 1:1$, and $\dfrac{HK}{KF} = \dfrac{m_F}{m_H} = \dfrac{3}{3} = 1:1$.

Example 8. Quadrilateral $ABCD$ circumscribed a circle as shown. Tangent points are $M, N, P,$ and Q on AB, BC, CD and $DA,$ respectively. Let 3, 6, 4, 2 be the lengths of the line segments shown. MP and NQ meet at Z. Calculate $MZ : ZP$ and $QZ : ZN$.

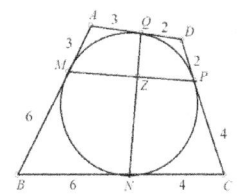

Solution: 3/2 and 1/2.
We assign the mass value 3 to point C.
$m_D = 6$. $m_A = 4$. $m_P = 9$.
$m_B = 2$.
$m_M = 6$.
$m_N = 5$.
$m_Q = 10$.

Thus $MZ : ZP = m_P / m_M = 9/6 = 3/2$.
Similarly, $QZ : ZN = m_N / m_Q = 5/10 = 1/2$.

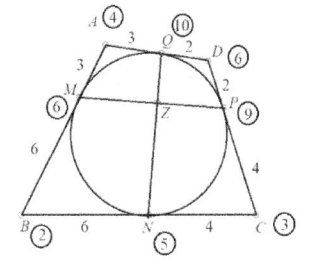

Example 9. Let $D\text{-}ABC$ be a regular tetrahedron (triangular pyramid) as shown. E, F, H, G are centroids of triangles $BCD, ACD, ABC,$ and ABD, respectively. Connect DH and AE and DH and AE meet at J. What is the ratio of DJ/JH?

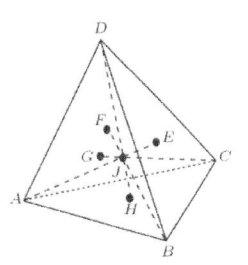

Solution: 3 : 1.
Assign the mass values 1, 1, 1, 1 to $A, B, C,$ and D.

127

The Mass Points Method   Chapter 6. Quadrilaterals and Space Problems

Connect AH and extend it to meet BC at M.

Since H is the centroid of triangle ABC, $AH : HM = 2 : 1$.
Thus $m_M = 2$ and $m_H = 3$.

So $DJ/JH = m_H/m_D = 3 : 1$.

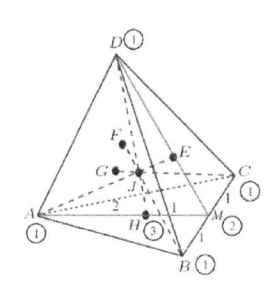

Example 10. D-ABC is a tetrahedron. Let E be in AB such that $AE : EB = 1 : 2$. Let H be in BC such that $BH : HC = 1 : 2$. Let AH intersect CE at K. Let M be the midpoint of DK and let HM intersect AD at L. Find $AL : LD$.

Solution: $AL : LD = 7 : 4$.
We can label each line segment and assign mass 1 to C.

Then we get $m_B = 2$, $m_A = 4$, $m_H = 3$, $m_K = 7$, $m_D = 7$.

We then find $\dfrac{AL}{LD} = \dfrac{m_D}{m_A} = \dfrac{7}{4}$.

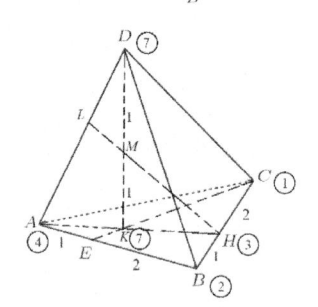

Example 11. D-ABC is a tetrahedron. Let E be in AB such that $AE : AB = 1 : 3$. Let H be in BC such that $BH : HC = 1 : 2$. Let AH intersect CE at K. Let M be a point of DK and let HM intersect AD at L. Find $DM : MK$ if $AL : LD = 5 : 2$.

Solution: $7 : 10$.

We can label each line segment and assign mass 1 to C.

Then we get $m_B = 2$, $m_A = 4$, $m_H = 3$, $m_K = 7$, $m_D = 10$.

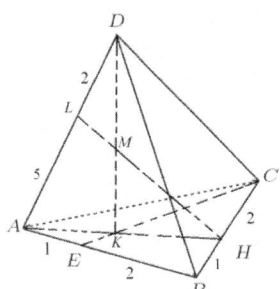

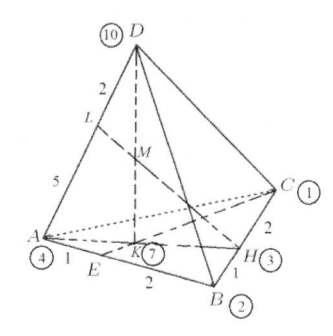

The Mass Points Method   Chapter 6. Quadrilaterals and Space Problems

We then find $\dfrac{DM}{MK} = \dfrac{m_K}{m_D} = \dfrac{7}{10}$.

Example 12. D-ABC is a tetrahedron. Let E be in AB such that $EB : AB = 2 : 3$. Let H be in BC such that $BH : BC = 1 : 3$. Let AH intersect CE at K. Let M be a point of DK and let HM intersect AD at L. Find $HM : HL$ if $AL : LD = 5 : 2$.

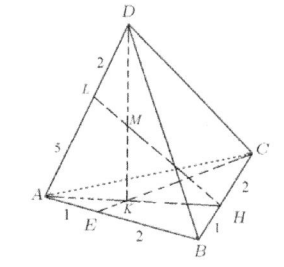

Solution: 14 : 17.
We can label each line segment and assign mass 1 to C.

Then we get $m_B = 2$, $m_A = 4$, $m_D = 10$, $m_H = 3$, $m_K = 7$, $m_L = 14$, $m_M = 17$.

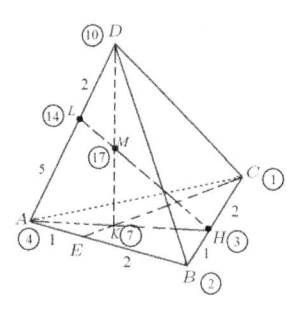

We then find $\dfrac{HM}{HL} = \dfrac{m_L}{m_M} = \dfrac{14}{17}$.

Example 13. Let $PABC$ be a right triangular pyramid. That is, the pyramid's base $\triangle ABC$ is an equilateral triangle, and the altitude from P goes through the centroid G of $\triangle ABC$. A plane intersects PA, PB, PC, and PG at points D, E, F, and H such that $\dfrac{PD}{DA} = \dfrac{2}{3}$, $\dfrac{PE}{EB} = \dfrac{3}{2}$, and $\dfrac{PF}{FC} = \dfrac{4}{1}$, respectively. Find the value of $\dfrac{PH}{HG}$.

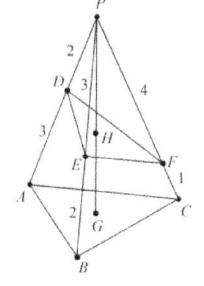

Solution: $\dfrac{36}{29}$.

The Mass Points Method   Chapter 6. Quadrilaterals and Space Problems

We can label each line segment and assign mass 12 to C.

Then we get $m_{P_{PC}} = 3$, $m_B = 12$, $m_A = 12$, $m_{P_{PA}} = 18$, $m_{P_{PB}} = 8$. $m_P = m_{P_{PC}} + m_{P_{PA}} + m_{P_{PB}} = 3 + 1 + 8 = 29$.

We connect BG and extend it to meet AC at K. $m_K = 24$, $m_G = 36$.

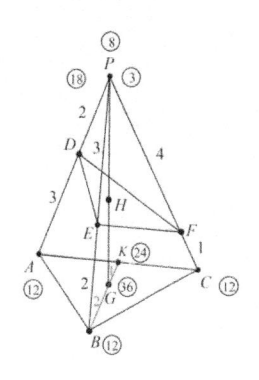

We then find $\dfrac{PH}{HG} = \dfrac{m_G}{m_P} = \dfrac{36}{29}$.

Example 14. Let $PABC$ be a right triangular pyramid. That is, the pyramid's base $\triangle ABC$ is an equilateral triangle, and the altitude from P goes through the centroid G of $\triangle ABC$. A plane intersects PA, PB, PC, and PG at points D, E, F, and H such that $PD : DA = 1 : 2$, $PE : EB = 5 : 3$, and $PF : PC = 3 : 4$, respectively. Find the value of $GH : HP$.

Solution: 44/45.

We can label each line segment and assign mass 15 to C.

Then we get $m_{P_{PC}} = 5$, $m_B = 15$, $m_A = 15$, $m_{P_{PA}} = 30$, $m_{P_{PB}} = 9$. $m_P = m_{P_{PC}} + m_{P_{PA}} + m_{P_{PB}} = 5 + 30 + 9 = 44$.

We connect BG and extend it to meet AC at K. $m_K = 30$, $m_G = 45$.

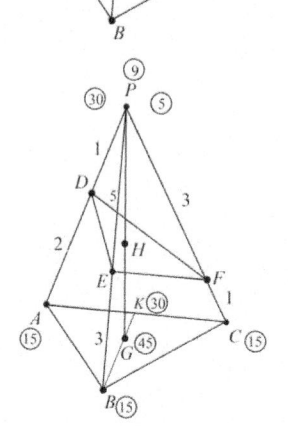

We then find $\dfrac{GH}{HP} = \dfrac{m_P}{m_G} = \dfrac{44}{45}$.

Example 15. (2013 Stanford Math Tournament) In tetrahedron $ABCD$, $AB = 4$, $CD = 7$, and $AC = AD = BC = BD = 5$. Let I_A, I_B, I_C, and I_D denote the incenters of the faces opposite vertices A, B, C, and D, respectively. It is provable that AI_A intersects BI_B at a point X, and CI_C intersects DI_D at a point Y. Compute XY.

The Mass Points Method Chapter 6. Quadrilaterals and Space Problems

Solution: $\frac{\sqrt{35}}{72}$.

First, we make some preliminary observations. Let M be the midpoint of AB and N be the midpoint of CD. We see that I_A and I_B lie on isosceles triangle ABN, since AN and BN are angle bisectors of $\angle CAD$ and $\angle CBD$, respectively. This shows that AI_A and BI_B are coplanar, so they intersect. Moreover, by symmetry, X must lie on MN. Analogous facts hold for triangle CDM and its associated points: in particular, Y also lies on MN.

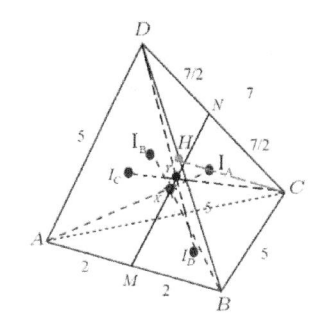

Now, we use mass points to determine the location of X on MN.

We connect CI_A and extend it to meet BD at H. Then $\frac{DH}{BH} = \frac{CD}{CB} = \frac{7}{5}$.

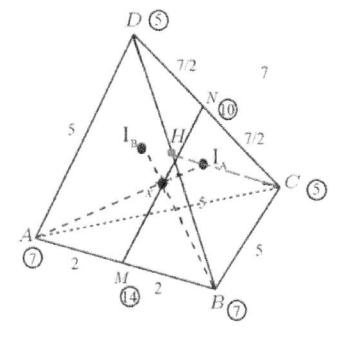

We assign the mass value 5 for point C, $m_C = 5$. We get $m_D = 5$. Then we calculate $\frac{DH}{BH} = \frac{m_B}{m_D} = \frac{7}{5} \quad \Rightarrow \quad m_B = \frac{7}{5} m_D = 7$. Thus $m_A = 7$.
$m_M = 14, m_N = 10.\ m_X = 24$.
Thus $\frac{MX}{MN} = \frac{m_N}{m_X} = \frac{10}{24} = \frac{5}{12}$.

Now, we use mass points to determine the location of Y on MN.

We connect BI_D and extend it to meet AC at G. Then $\frac{AG}{CG} = \frac{AB}{BC} = \frac{4}{5}$.

As we did before, we assign the mass value 5 for point C, $m_C = 5$. We get $m_D = 5$. Then we calculate $\frac{AG}{CG} = \frac{m_C}{m_A} = \frac{4}{5} \quad \Rightarrow \quad m_A = \frac{5}{4} m_C = \frac{25}{4}$. Thus $m_B = \frac{25}{4}$.

$m_M = 2 \times \frac{25}{4} = \frac{25}{2}, m_N = 10.\ m_Y = \frac{45}{2}$.
Thus $\frac{MY}{MN} = \frac{m_N}{m_Y} = \frac{10}{\frac{45}{2}} = \frac{4}{9}$.

131

The Mass Points Method   Chapter 6. Quadrilaterals and Space Problems

Thus $\frac{XY}{MN} = \frac{MX}{MN} - \frac{MY}{MN} = \frac{5}{12} - \frac{4}{9} = \frac{1}{36}$.

By Pythagorean Thereon,

$CM = \sqrt{CB^2 - BM^2} = \sqrt{5^2 - 2^2} = \sqrt{21}$.

$MN = \sqrt{CM^2 - CN^2} = \sqrt{21 - (\frac{7}{2})^2} = \frac{\sqrt{35}}{2}$.

$XY = \frac{\sqrt{35}}{72}$.

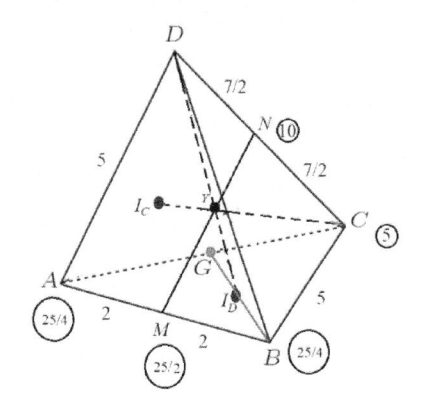

Example 16. (2018 Mathcounts State Sprint Problem 30) In right pyramid $PABCD$, $ABCD$ is a square with sides of length 2 and the distance from P to the center of square $ABCD$ is 1. A plane intersects the pyramid at A and intersects edges PB, PC and PD at points B', C' and D', respectively. If $B'B/PB = 1/4$, and $D'D/PD = 1/5$, what is the value of the ratio $C'C/PC$? Express your answer as a common fraction.

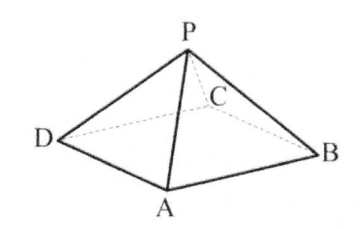

Solution: $\frac{7}{19}$.

We can label each line segment and assign a mass of 12 to B.

Then we get $m_C = m_A = m_D = 12$.

We calculate $m_{P_{PB}} = 4$, $m_{P_{PD}} = 3$.
We know that $m_{P_{PA}} = 0$.

We let $m_{P_{PC}} = x$.

$m_{P_{PC}} + m_{P_{PA}} = m_{P_{PB}} + m_{P_{PD}}$ $\Rightarrow$ $x + 0 = 4 + 3$.

$m_{P_{PC}} = x = 7$.

$m_{C'} \; 7 + 12 = 19$.

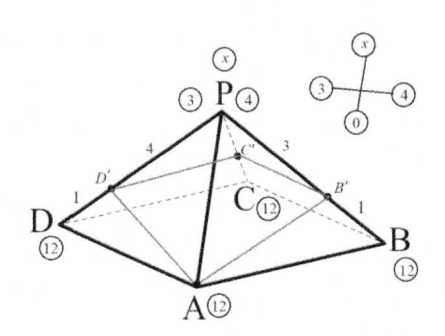

132

The Mass Points Method   Chapter 6. Quadrilaterals and Space Problems

We then find $\dfrac{CC'}{PC} = \dfrac{m_{P_{PC}}}{m_{C'}} = \dfrac{7}{19}$.

Example 17. In right pyramid *PABCD*, *ABCD* is a square with sides of length 4 and the distance from *P* to the center of square *ABCD* is 1. A plane intersects edges *PA*, *PB*, *PC* and *PD* at points *B'*, *C'* and *D'*, respectively. If *A'A/PA* = 1/3, *B'B/PB* = 1/4, and *D'D/PD* = 1/5, what is the value of the ratio *C'C/PC* ? Express your answer as a common fraction.

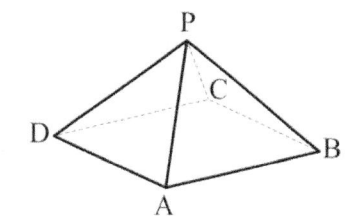

Solution: $\dfrac{1}{13}$.

We can label each line segment and assign a mass of 12 to *B*.

Then we get $m_C = m_A = m_D = 12$.

We calculate $m_{P_{PB}} = 4$, $m_{P_{PD}} = 3$, $m_{P_{PA}} = 6$.

We let $m_{P_{PC}} = x$.

$m_{P_{PC}} + m_{P_{PA}} = m_{P_{PB}} + m_{P_{PD}}$ ⇒ $x + 6 = 4 + 3$.

$m_{P_{PC}} = x = 1$. $m_{C'} = 1 + 12 = 13$.

We then find $\dfrac{CC'}{PC} = \dfrac{m_{P_{PC}}}{m_{C'}} = \dfrac{1}{13}$.

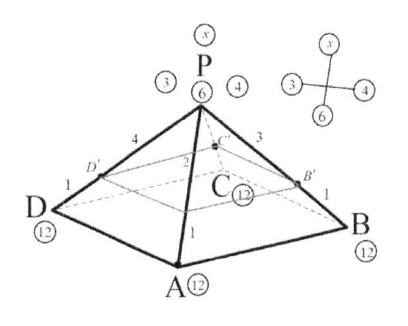

Example 18. Let *P-ABCD* be a pyramid on square base *ABCD* with *E*, *F*, *G*, *H* the respective midpoints of *AB*, *AD*, *DC*, and *CB*; and let *E'*, *F'*, be the respective centroids of △*PCD*, and △*PBC*, respectively. If *EE'* and *FF'* meets at *K*, find the ratio of *EK/ KE'*.

Solution: $\dfrac{3}{2}$.

We can label each line segment and assign a mass of 1 to *B*.

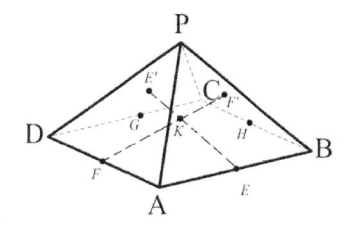

133

The Mass Points Method   Chapter 6. Quadrilaterals and Space Problems

Then we get $m_C = m_A = m_D = 1$, and $m_E = 2$.

We connect PE' and extend it to meet DC at G.

We know that $\dfrac{PE'}{GE'} = \dfrac{2}{1}$.

We alos know that $m_G = m_D + m_C = 1 + 1 = 2$

Thus $m_{E'} = 3$.

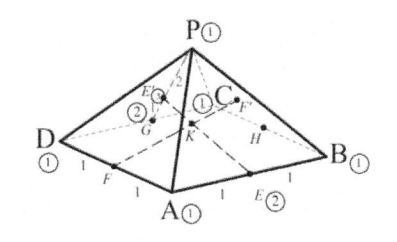

We then find $\dfrac{EK}{KE'} = \dfrac{m_{E'}}{m_E} = \dfrac{3}{2}$.

The Mass Points Method   Chapter 6. Quadrilaterals and Space Problems

Chapter 6. Problems

Problem 1. In rectangle *ABCD*, shown here, point *M* is the midpoint of side *BC*, and point *N* lies on *CD* such that $DN : NC = 2 : 5$. Segment *BN* intersects *AM* and *AC* at points *R* and *S*, respectively. If $NS : SR : RB = x : y : z$, where *x*, *y* and *z* are positive integers, what is the minimum possible value of $x + y + z$?

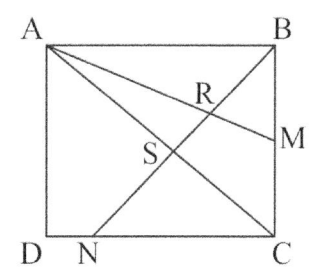

Problem 2. In parallelogram *ABCD*, shown here, point *F* is the midpoint of side *C* and point *E* is on the *AB* such that $\dfrac{AE}{BE} = \dfrac{2}{3}$. *AF* meets *DE* at *G* and *BD* at *H*. Find the area of quadrilateral *BHGE* if the area of *ABCD* is 180.

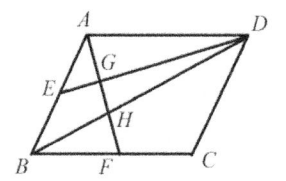

Problem 3. In trapezoid *ABCD*, $AB = 4CD$ and *AB* // *CD*. *E* is the midpoint of the diagonal *AC*. *BE* meets *AD* at *F*. Find the value of $AF : FD$. Express your answer as a common fraction.

Problem 4. Triangle *ABC* with $AB = 50$ and $AC = 10$ has area 120. Let *D* be the midpoint of *AB*, and let E be the midpoint of *AC*. The angle bisector of *BAC* intersects *DE* and *BC* at *F* and *G*, respectively. What is the area of quadrilateral *CEFG*?

(A) 60   (B) 65   (C) 70   (D) 75   (E) 80

The Mass Points Method   Chapter 6. Quadrilaterals and Space Problems

Problem 5. If $ABCD$ is a 4×4 square, E is the midpoint of $\overline{AB}$, F is the midpoint of $\overline{BC}$, $\overline{AF}$ and $\overline{DE}$ intersect at I, and $\overline{BD}$ and $\overline{AF}$ intersect at H, then the area of triangle DHI is

(A) $\dfrac{3}{2}$ (B) $\dfrac{6}{5}$ (C) $\dfrac{32}{15}$ (D) $\dfrac{17}{15}$ (E) $\dfrac{5}{3}$

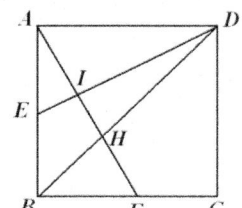

Problem 6. $ABCD$ is a trapezoid with $CD = 2AB$. Let E be in BC such that $BE : EC = 2: 5$. F is the intersection of the diagonals. Extend EF to meet AD at G. Find $EF : FG$ and $AG : GD$.

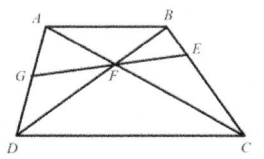

Problem 7. In quadrilateral $ABCD$, E, F, G, H are the points on AB, CB, CD, and AD, respectively such that $AE : EB = 1 : 2$, $BF : FC = 2 : 1$, $CG : GD = 1 : 1$, and $DH : HA = 1 : 1$. Let EG intersect HF at K. Find the numerical values of $GK : KE$ and $HK : KF$.

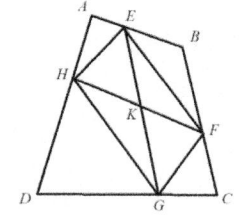

Problem 8. Quadrilateral $ABCD$ circumscribed a circle as shown. Tangent points are $M, N, P,$ and Q on AB, BC, CD and DA, respectively. Let a, b, c, d be the lengths of the line segments shown. MP and NQ meet at Z. Calculate $MZ : ZP$ and $QZ : ZN$.

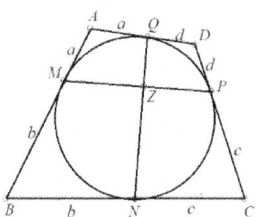

136

The Mass Points Method   Chapter 6. Quadrilaterals and Space Problems

Problem 9. Consider a tetrahedron $ABCD$ in space. Let P, Q, R, and S be, respectively, the centroids of $\triangle ABC$, $\triangle ABD$, $\triangle ACD$, and $\triangle BCD$. Prove that the line segments AS, BR, CQ, and DP all intersect in a common point T. What are the ratios $AT/TS + DT/TP + BT/TR + CT/TQ$?

Problem 10. D-ABC is a tetrahedron. Let E be in AB such that $AE : EB = 1 : 2$. Let H be in BC such that $BH : HC = 1 : 2$. Let AH intersect CE at K. Let M be the midpoint of DK and let HM intersect AD at L. Find $LM : MH$.

Problem 11. D-ABC is a tetrahedron. Let E be in AB such that $AE : AB = 1 : 3$. Let H be in BC such that $BH : HC = 1 : 2$. Let AH intersect CE at K. Let M be a point of DK and let HM intersect AD at L. Find $LM : LH$ if $AL : LD = 5 : 2$.

137

The Mass Points Method   Chapter 6. Quadrilaterals and Space Problems

Problem 12. *D-ABC* is a tetrahedron. Let *E* be on side *AB* such that *AE : EB* = 1 : 2. Let *H* be on side *BC* such that *BH : HC* = 1 : 2. Let *AH* intersect *CE* at point *K*. Let *M* be the midpoint of *DK* and let *HM* intersect *AD* at *L*. Find *LM : LH*.

Problem 13. Let *PABC* be a right triangular pyramid. That is, the pyramid's base $\triangle ABC$ is an equilateral triangle, and the altitude from *P* goes through the centroid *G* of $\triangle ABC$. A plane intersects *PA*, *PB*, *PC*, and *PG* at points *D, E, F*, and *H* such that *PD : PA* = 2 : 5, *PE : PB* = 3 : 5, and *PF : PC* = 4 : 5, respectively. Find the value of *GH : GP*.

Problem 14. Let *PABC* be a right triangular pyramid. That is, the pyramid's base $\triangle ABC$ is an equilateral triangle, and the altitude from *P* goes through the centroid *G* of $\triangle ABC$. A plane intersects *PA*, *PB*, *PC*, and *PG* at points *D, E, F*, and *H* such that *PD : PA* = 1 : 3, *PE : PB* = 5 : 8, and *PF : PC* = 3 : 4, respectively. Find the value of *PH : PG*.

Problem 15. In right pyramid *PABCD*, *ABCD* is a square with sides of length 8 and the distance from *P* to the center of square *ABCD* is 3. A plane intersects the pyramid at *A* and intersects edges *PB*, *PC* and *PD* at points *B′*, *C′* and *D′*, respectively. If *B′B/ B′P* = 1/4, and *DD′ / D′P* = 1/5, what

138

The Mass Points Method   Chapter 6. Quadrilaterals and Space Problems

is the value of the ratio $CC'/C'P$? Express your answer as a common fraction.

Problem 16. In right pyramid $PABCD$, $ABCD$ is a square with sides of length 4 and the distance from P to the center of square $ABCD$ is 1. A plane intersects edges PA, PB, PC and PD at points B', C' and D', respectively. If $AA'/A'P = 2/3$, $BB'/B'P = 3/4$, and $D'D/D'P = 1/3$, what is the value of the ratio $C'C/PC$? Express your answer as a common fraction.

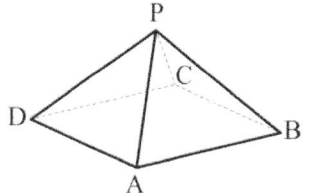

Problem 17. The base of a pyramid $SABCD$ is a parallelogram $ABCD$. A plane intersects the sides SA, SB, SC, and SD at points E, F, G, and H, respectively. Given that $\dfrac{SE}{SA} = \dfrac{3}{5}$, $\dfrac{SF}{SB} = \dfrac{1}{3}$, and $\dfrac{SG}{SC} = \dfrac{1}{5}$, find $\dfrac{SH}{SD}$.

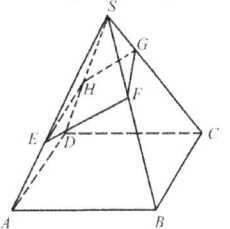

The Mass Points Method   Chapter 6. Quadrilaterals and Space Problems

Chapter 6. Solutions

Problem 1. Solution: 228.
$\triangle ABS \sim \triangle CNS$. Since $DN : NC = 2 : 5$, $NC/AB = 5/7$. Thus $NS/SB = 5 : 7$ and $AS/SC = 7 : 5$.
We assign the mass value of 7 to point C.
$m_C = 7$, $m_B = 7$, $m_A = 5$, $m_S = 12$.
Thus $y : z = SR/RB = 7 : 12$.
Since we only want to find the ratio, we let $y = 7$ and $z = 12$.
$(y + z)/x = 7/5 \quad \Rightarrow \quad x = 95/7$.
$x : y : z = 95/7 : 7 : 12 = 95/7 : 49/7 : 84/7$.
The minimum possible value of $x + y + z$ is $95 + 49 + 84 = 228$.

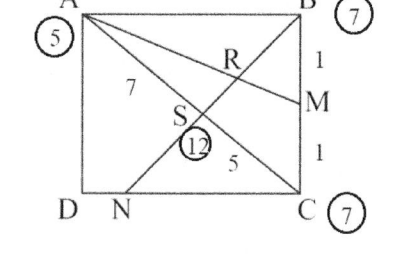

Problem 2. Solution: 21.
Since $ABCD$ is a parallelogram, $AD // BC$, triangle ADH is similar to triangle FBH.
$$\frac{AD}{BF} = \frac{DH}{BH} = \frac{2}{1}.$$
We label each line segment as shown.
Then we assign the mass value of 2 to point B.
$m_D = 1$, $m_A = 3$, $m_E = 5$, $m_G = 6$, and $m_H = 3$.
$$\frac{S_{\triangle ABH}}{S_{\triangle ABD}} = \frac{BH}{BD} = \frac{m_D}{m_H} = \frac{1}{3} \quad \Rightarrow \quad S_{\triangle ABH} = \frac{1}{3} S_{\triangle ABD} = \frac{1}{6} S_{ABCD} = 30.$$
$$\frac{S_{\triangle AEG}}{S_{\triangle AED}} = \frac{EG}{ED} = \frac{m_D}{m_G} = \frac{1}{6} \quad \Rightarrow \quad S_{\triangle AEG} = \frac{1}{6} S_{\triangle AED} = \frac{1}{20} S_{ABCD} = 9.$$
Therefore $S_{BHGE} = S_{\triangle ABH} - S_{\triangle AEG} = 30 - 9 = 21$.

Problem 3. Solution: $\dfrac{4}{3}$.

Extend CD and BF to meet at G. Since $CG // AB$,
$\triangle ABE \sim \triangle CGE$. So

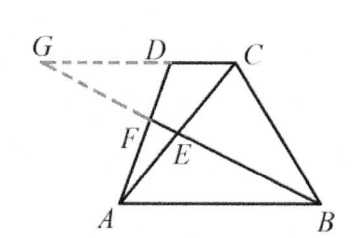

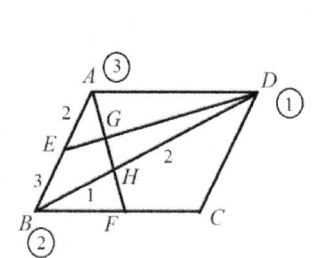

140

The Mass Points Method   Chapter 6. Quadrilaterals and Space Problems

$\dfrac{CG}{AB} = \dfrac{CE}{AE} = 1 \Rightarrow CG = AB \Rightarrow GD + CD = 4CD \Rightarrow GD = 3CD$

We label each line segment as shown.
Then we assign the mass value of 3 to point A.
Then we calculate: $m_C = 3$, $m_G = 1$, $m_D = 4$.

$\dfrac{AF}{FD} = \dfrac{m_D}{m_A} = \dfrac{4}{3}$.

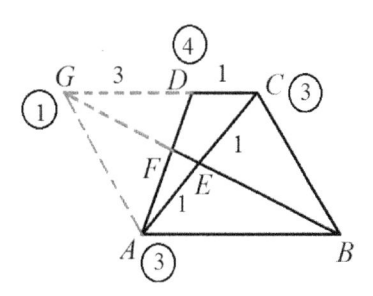

Problem 4. Solution: (D).

$S_{\triangle AED} = \dfrac{1}{2} AE \times AD = \dfrac{1}{2} \times 5 \times 25 \sin(2\alpha)$ \hfill (1)

$S_{\triangle ACB} = \dfrac{1}{2} AC \times AB = \dfrac{1}{2} \times 10 \times 50 \sin(2\alpha)$ \hfill (2)

(1) ÷ (2): $S_{\triangle AED} = \dfrac{1}{4} \times S_{\triangle ACB} = 30$

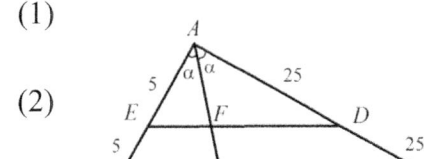

We label each line segment as shown.
Then we assign the mass value of 1 to point B. Then we calculate: $m_C = 5$, $m_G = 6$, $m_{A_{AB}} = 1$, $m_D = 2$, $m_{A_{AC}} = 5$, $m_E = 10$, $m_F = 12$, $m_{A_{AG}} = 6$.

$\dfrac{S_{\triangle AEF}}{S_{\triangle AED}} = \dfrac{EF}{DE} = \dfrac{m_D}{m_F} = \dfrac{2}{12} = \dfrac{1}{6}$

$\Rightarrow \quad S_{\triangle AEF} = \dfrac{1}{6} \times 30 = 5$.

$\dfrac{S_{\triangle ACG}}{S_{\triangle ABC}} = \dfrac{CG}{BC} = \dfrac{m_B}{m_G} = \dfrac{1}{6}$

$\Rightarrow \quad S_{\triangle ACG} = \dfrac{1}{6} \times 120 = 20$

$S_{CEFG} = S_{\triangle ACG} - S_{\triangle AEF} = 20 - 5 = 15$.

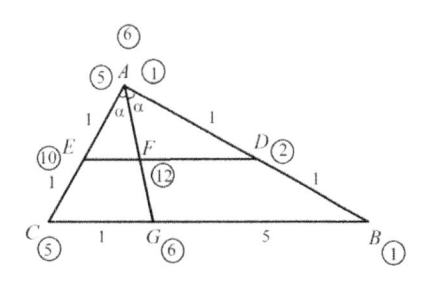

Problem 5. Solution: (C).

Since $\triangle ADH \sim \triangle FBH$, $\dfrac{DH}{BH} = \dfrac{AD}{BF} = \dfrac{1}{2}$.

141

The Mass Points Method   Chapter 6. Quadrilaterals and Space Problems

We label each line segments and assign the value 1 to the point D and calculate the masses for each point as shown.

$$\frac{S_{\triangle ADH}}{S_{\triangle ABD}} = \frac{DH}{BD} = \frac{2}{3}$$

$$\Rightarrow \quad S_{\triangle ADH} = \frac{2}{3} S_{\triangle ABD} = \frac{2}{3} \times \frac{4 \times 4}{2} = \frac{16}{3}$$

$$\frac{S_{\triangle DHI}}{S_{\triangle AHD}} = \frac{HI}{AH} = \frac{m_A}{m_I} = \frac{2}{5}$$

$$\Rightarrow \quad S_{\triangle DHI} = \frac{2}{5} S_{\triangle AHD} = \frac{2}{5} \times \frac{16}{3} = \frac{32}{15}.$$

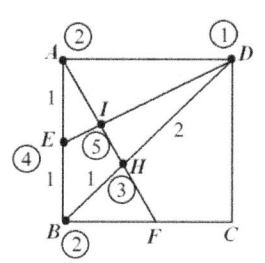

Problem 6. Solution: 13 : 14 and 5 : 8.
Since $AB : DC = 1 : 2$, we have $BF : FD = AF : FC = 1 : 2$.
So we can label each line segment and assign mass 4 to C.

Then we get $m_A = 8$, $m_B = 6$, $m_D = 5$, $m_G = 13$, $m_E = 14$.

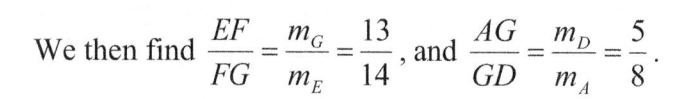

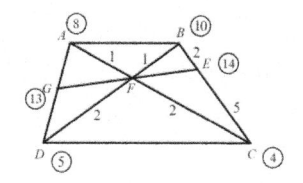

We then find $\dfrac{EF}{FG} = \dfrac{m_G}{m_E} = \dfrac{13}{14}$, and $\dfrac{AG}{GD} = \dfrac{m_D}{m_A} = \dfrac{5}{8}$.

Problem 7. Solution: 3 : 4 and 3 : 4.
We can label each line segment and assign mass 2 to C.

Then we get $m_B = 1$, $m_F = 3$, $m_A = 2$, $m_E = 3$, $m_D = 2$, $m_H = 4$.

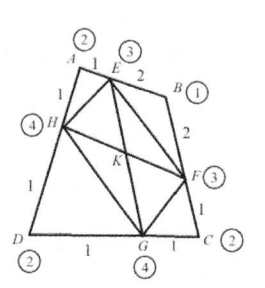

We then find $\dfrac{GK}{KE} = \dfrac{m_E}{m_G} = \dfrac{3}{4}$, and $\dfrac{HK}{KF} = \dfrac{m_F}{m_H} = \dfrac{3}{4}$.

Problem 8. Solution:
We assign the mass value d to point C.
$m_D = c$. $m_A = dc/a$. $m_P = d + c$.

The Mass Points Method   Chapter 6. Quadrilaterals and Space Problems

$m_B = dc/b$.
$m_M = dc/a + dc/b$.
$m_N = dc/b + d$.
$m_Q = dc/a + c$.

Thus $MZ : ZP = m_P/m_M = (d + c)/(dc/a + dc/b) = ab(d + c)/[dc(a + b)]$.

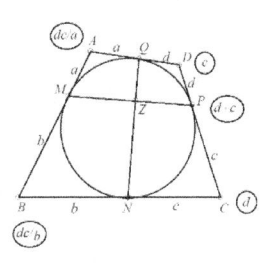

Similarly, $QZ : ZN = m_N/m_Q = (dc/b + d)/[dc/a + c)] = ad(b + c)/[bc(a + d)]$.

Problem 9. Solution: 12.
Assign the mass values 1, 1, 1, 1 to A, B, C, and D.

Let M be the midpoint of BC. Connect AM, DM. Since P and S are the centroids, A, P, and M are collinear, and D, S, and M are collinear

Since P is the centroid of triangle ABC, $AP : PM = 2 : 1$.
Similarly, $DS : SM = 2 : 1$.
Thus $m_M = 2$ and $m_P = 3$. $m_S = 3$.
$AT/TS = m_S/m_A = 3/1$.
$DT/TP = m_P/m_D = 3/1$.
Similarly, we have $BT/TR = CT/TQ = 3/1$.
$AT/TS + DT/TP + BT/TR + CT/TQ = 12$.

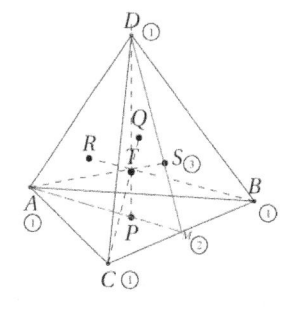

Problem 10. Solution: 3 : 11.
We can label each line segment and assign mass 1 to C.

Then we get $m_B = 2$, $m_A = 4$, $m_H = 3$, $m_K = 7$, $m_D = 7$.

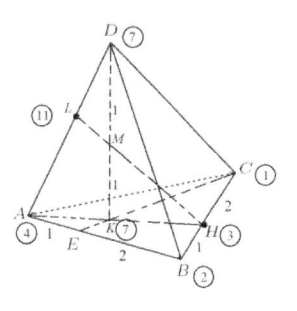

We then find $\dfrac{LM}{MH} = \dfrac{m_H}{m_L} = \dfrac{3}{11}$.

Problem 11. Solution: 3 : 14.

143

The Mass Points Method Chapter 6. Quadrilaterals and Space Problems

We can label each line segment and assign mass 1 to C.

Then we get $m_B = 2$, $m_A = 4$, $m_D = 10$, $m_H = 3$, $m_K = 7$, $m_L = 14$, $m_M = 17$.

We then find $\dfrac{LM}{LH} = \dfrac{m_H}{m_M} = \dfrac{3}{14}$.

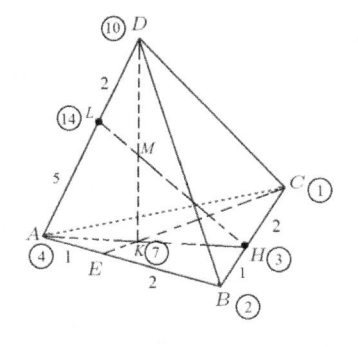

Problem 12. Solution: 3 : 14.
We can label each line segment and assign mass 1 to C.

Then we get $m_B = 2$, $m_A = 4$, $m_H = 3$, $m_K = 7$, $m_D = 7$.
$m_L = 11$, $m_M = 14$.

We then find $\dfrac{LM}{LH} = \dfrac{m_H}{m_M} = \dfrac{3}{14}$.

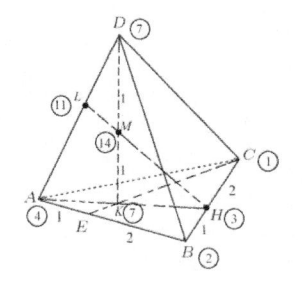

Problem 13. Solution: $\dfrac{29}{65}$.

We can label each line segment and assign mass 12 to C.

Then we get $m_{P_{PC}} = 3$, $m_B = 12$, $m_A = 12$, $m_{P_{PA}} = 18$, $m_{P_{PB}} = 8$.
$m_P = m_{P_{PC}} + m_{P_{PA}} + m_{P_{PB}} = 3 + 1 + 8 = 29$.

We connect BG and extend it to meet AC at K. $m_K = 24$, $m_G = 36$.

We then find $\dfrac{GH}{GP} = \dfrac{m_P}{m_H} = \dfrac{29}{65}$.

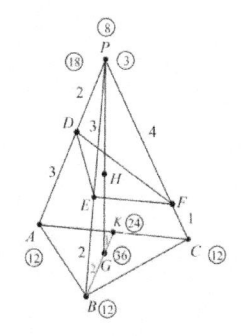

The Mass Points Method   Chapter 6. Quadrilaterals and Space Problems

Problem 14. Solution: 45/99. 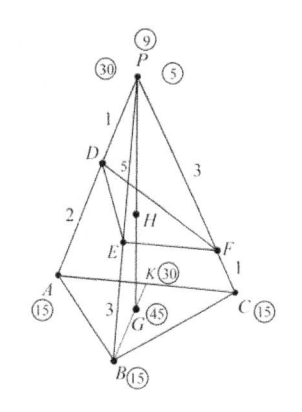
We can label each line segment and assign a mass of 15 to C.

Then we get $m_{P_{PC}} = 5$, $m_B = 15$, $m_A = 15$, $m_{P_{PA}} = 30$, $m_{P_{PB}} = 9$. $m_P = m_{P_{PC}} + m_{P_{PA}} + m_{P_{PB}} = 5 + 30 + 9 = 44$.
We connect BG and extend it to meet AC at K. $m_K = 30$, $m_G = 45$, $m_H = 44 + 45 = 99$,
We then find $\dfrac{PH}{PG} = \dfrac{m_G}{m_H} = \dfrac{45}{99}$.

Problem 15. Solution: $\dfrac{9}{20}$.

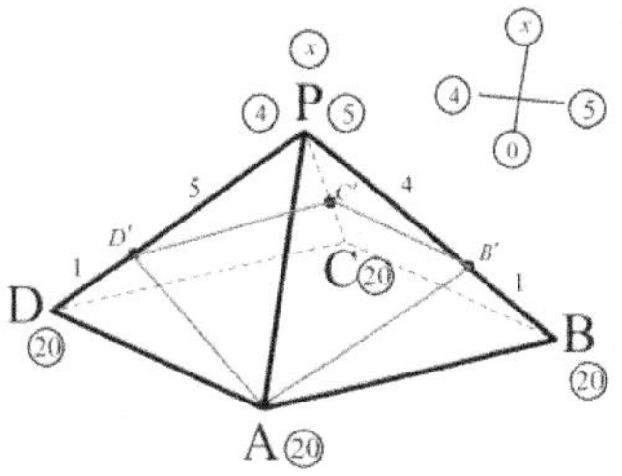

We can label each line segment and assign a mass of 20 to B.

Then we get $m_C = m_A = m_D = 20$.

We calculate $m_{P_{PB}} = 5$, $m_{P_{PD}} = 4$.
We know that $m_{P_{PA}} = 0$.
We let $m_{P_{PC}} = x$.
$m_{P_{PC}} + m_{P_{PA}} = m_{P_{PB}} + m_{P_{PD}}$ $\Rightarrow$ $x + 0 = 4 + 5$.
$m_{P_{PC}} = x = 9$.
We then find $\dfrac{CC'}{C'P} = \dfrac{m_{P_{PC}}}{m_C} = \dfrac{9}{20}$.

Problem 16. Solution: $\dfrac{1}{13}$.

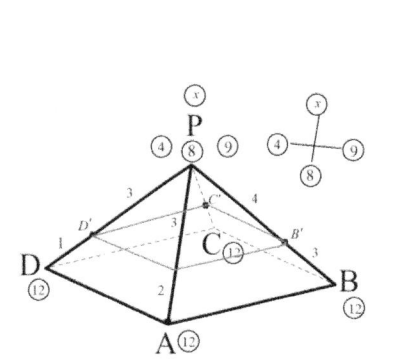

We can label each line segment and assign a mass of 12 to B.

Then we get $m_C = m_A = m_D = 12$.

145

The Mass Points Method   Chapter 6. Quadrilaterals and Space Problems

We calculate $m_{P_{PB}} = 9$, $m_{P_{PD}} = 4$, $m_{P_{PA}} = 8$.

We let $m_{P_{PC}} = x$.

$m_{P_{PC}} + m_{P_{PA}} = m_{P_{PB}} + m_{P_{PD}} \Rightarrow x + 8 = 4 + 9$.

$m_{P_{PC}} = x = 5$. $m_{C'} = 5 + 12 = 17$.

We then find $\dfrac{CC'}{PC} = \dfrac{m_{P_{PC}}}{m_{C'}} = \dfrac{5}{17}$.

Problem 17. Solution: $\dfrac{3}{11}$.

We can label each line segment and assign a mass of 3 to B.

Then we get $m_C = m_A = m_D = 3$.

We calculate $m_{S_{SB}} = 6$, $m_{S_{SA}} = 2$, $m_{S_{SC}} = 12$.

We let $m_{S_{SD}} = x$.

$m_{S_{SA}} + m_{S_{SC}} = m_{S_{SB}} + m_{S_{SD}} \Rightarrow x + 6 = 2 + 12$.

$m_{S_{SD}} = x = 8$. $m_H = 8 + 3 = 11$.

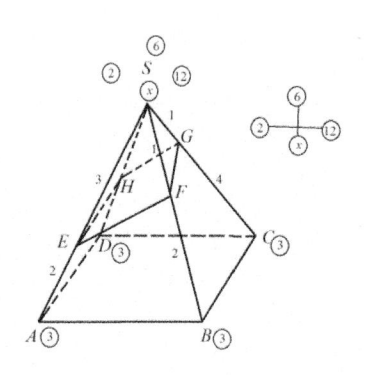

$\dfrac{SH}{SD} = \dfrac{m_D}{m_H} = \dfrac{3}{11}$.

Index

A
angle, 70, 83
area, 1, 61, 77, 79, 80, 82, 86, 88, 90, 95, 99, 100, 108
average, 1

B
base, 35

C
center, 1, 3, 9, 10, 16, 17, 21, 45, 49, 59, 62, 63, 64, 65, 66, 72, 73, 82, 84, 85, 106
common fraction, 6, 20, 21, 22, 23, 26, 31, 32, 33, 62, 63, 64, 70, 71, 81, 86, 99, 100

E
equation, 1

F
fraction, 6, 20, 21, 22, 23, 26, 31, 32, 33, 35, 62, 63, 64, 70, 71, 81, 86, 99

I
integers, 47, 50, 54, 83, 95
intersection, 1, 3, 31, 32, 33, 34, 45

L
line, 1, 3, 5, 6, 12, 20, 21, 23, 24, 25, 26, 35, 36, 37, 38, 39, 40, 41, 42, 43, 44, 45, 48, 50, 57, 58, 62, 63, 64, 65, 66, 72, 73, 74, 77, 78, 80, 81, 82, 83, 84, 85, 86, 94, 104, 105, 106, 107, 114, 116

line segment, 1, 20, 21, 23, 24, 25, 26, 35, 36, 37, 38, 39, 40, 41, 42, 43, 44, 45, 48, 50, 57, 58, 63, 64, 66, 72, 73, 74, 77, 78, 80, 81, 82, 83, 84, 85, 86, 94, 104, 105, 106, 107, 114, 116

M
median, 6, 7, 8, 10, 14, 20, 25, 47, 48, 54, 55, 77, 87, 91, 101
midpoint, 31, 32, 33, 65, 100

P
parallel, 35, 95
perpendicular, 100
point, 1, 2, 3, 5, 6, 10, 17, 20, 22, 23, 24, 25, 26, 27, 31, 32, 33, 34, 35, 36, 37, 38, 39, 40, 41, 42, 43, 44, 45, 47, 48, 49, 50, 56, 57, 58, 59, 60, 61, 62, 63, 64, 65, 66, 70, 72, 73, 74, 75, 77, 78, 80, 82, 83, 84, 85, 86, 88, 89, 90, 91, 94, 95, 99, 100, 104, 105, 107, 108, 114, 115, 116
proportion, 1
Pythagorean Theorem, 84, 85

Q
quadrilateral, 77, 79, 80, 81, 99, 100, 108

R
ratio, 2, 22, 23, 31, 35, 62, 63, 64, 70, 83, 84, 86, 95, 97, 100, 108
relatively prime, 83, 95
right triangle, 100, 106, 116

S
set, 36
similar, 95, 96, 97, 107

solution, 35, 95

T

transversal, 6, 22, 26, 37, 38, 39, 41, 42, 43, 44, 58, 60, 62, 63, 64, 70, 71

triangle, 10, 14, 25, 26, 31, 32, 33, 34, 35, 42, 47, 48, 54, 55, 61, 62, 63, 65, 70, 71, 77, 79, 83, 84, 86, 87, 88, 90, 95, 100, 107

V

vertex, 1, 5, 6

volume, 1

A List of Math Contest Preparation Books

1. Mathcounts Books and Practice Tests
Mathcounts Tips for Beginners
Twenty Problem Solving Skills for Mathcounts
Twenty More Problem Solving Skills
50 Mathcounts Lectures (3 Volumes)
50 Mathcounts Lectures Solutions (3 Volumes)
Mathcounts State Competitions Prep Books (5 Volumes)
Eleven Years Mathcounts Chapter Solutions
Eleven Years Mathcounts State Solutions
Eleven Years Mathcounts National Solutions
Mathcounts National Solutions (2011-2016)
Mathcounts Speed and Accuracy Practice Tests
Mathcounts Chapter Competition Practice
Mathcounts National Competition Practice
Twenty Mock Mathcounts Target Round Tests
Twenty Mock Mathcounts Sprint Round Tests

2. American Mathematics Examinations
AMC 8 Preparation Books (5 Volumes)
AMC 8 Practice Tests
AMC 10 Preparation Books (5 Volumes)
AMC 10 Practice Tests
50 AMC Lectures (4 Volumes)
50 AMC Problems (2 Volumes)
Fifty Lectures for AIME Volume 1, 2, 3

3. Math Competition Books Series
The Mass Points Method
Balls and Boxes
The Area Method
Problem Solving Using Cauthy's Inequalities
Problem Solving Using the Discriminant
The Completing the Square Method

4. Others
Algebra II Through Competitions
Geometry Through Competitions
ARML Preparation Volume 1

Printed in Great Britain
by Amazon